Anti-manipulation Regime in Korea

International Banking and Securities Law

Volume published in this Brill Research Perspective are listed at *brill.com/rpbs*

Anti-manipulation Regime in Korea

A Critique and Comparative Exploration

By

Min-woo Kang

BRILL

LEIDEN | BOSTON

Library of Congress Control Number: 2025930456

Typeface for the Latin, Greek, and Cyrillic scripts: "Brill". See and download: brill.com/brill-typeface.

ISSN 2405-6928
ISBN 978-90-04-49953-9 (paperback)
ISBN 978-90-04-50839-2 (e-book)
DOI 10.1163/9789004508392

This book is printed on acid-free paper and produced in a sustainable manner.

Contents

Anti-manipulation Regime in Korea: a Critique and Comparative Exploration

Min-woo Kang | ORCID: 0000-0001-9933-7508
Senior Fellow, Centre for Financial Law, Legal Research Institute of Korea University, Seoul, Korea

Abstract

Market manipulation is generally deemed an illicit activity that undermines market integrity and jeopardises investor interests, and is therefore prohibited in every jurisdiction. However, its lack of clarity of the legal standards hinders consistent and predictable law enforcement. Absent a principled approach to prohibitions, the Korean regime for market manipulation encounters this very problem. Furthermore, its two-tiered hierarchical system of law enforcement degrades the quality of regulatory performance. Additionally, the Korean law is silent on algorithmic and high-frequency trading activities that could have potentially manipulative effects on capital markets, leaving much responsibility on a self-regulatory organisation such as an exchange. This inquiry presents the analysis of these vexing issues by exploring the regulatory systems across major jurisdictions and their fits on the legal standards. In doing so, it argues the need for a revision of the anti-manipulation regime in Korea, offering some practical suggestions for improvement.

Keywords

market manipulation – high frequency and algorithmic trading – market disruption – fraud and deceit – misinformation

1 Introduction

One of the most salient challenges financial regulators are facing today is how to combat financial misconduct such as market manipulation, wherein an investor (or in concert with other traders) intervenes in the proper interplay of supply and demand for financial instruments to distort the price formation

 | DOI:10.1163/9789004508392_002

mechanism.[1] Market manipulation impairs 'the integrity of, and thereby undermines investor confidence in, securities and derivatives markets'; that is, it erodes the base of overarching objectives of financial regulation.[2] Thus, market manipulation is generally deemed an illicit activity, and it is prohibited in every jurisdiction.

Market manipulation is in fact not a new phenomenon.[3] Rather, it will be more accurate to say that manipulative trading and its regulation have always been in existence in securities markets since their inception. However, it is worth noting that more recent developments, namely fast-evolving market environments represented by advances in technology innovation (e.g., a fully automated electronic trading), cross-border market integration, the emergence of highly sophisticated products and the increasing participation of retail investors in equity markets have transformed market structures considerably, continuing to shape new trading landscapes.[4] Certainly, all these changes have significantly 'impacted the way in which trading on capital markets is conducted' and have provided traders with more incentives, means and opportunities for implementing manipulative schemes.[5] As demonstrated by the 2010 Flash Crash, during which US stock markets experienced a systemic intraday event, the evolution of trading technology, notably the widespread adoption of algorithmic and high-frequency trading (HFT), have contributed to the rising incidents of market manipulation.[6]

Indeed, reports of suspected manipulative trades made to the regulatory authorities in major jurisdictions are on the rise, suggesting that the risk and hazard of market manipulation is far from eradicated.[7] According to the EU

1 International Organisation of Securities Commissions (IOSCO), Investigating and Prosecuting Market Manipulation, Report of the Technical Committee of the IOSCO (May 2000) https://www.iosco.org/library/pubdocs/pdf/IOSCOPD103.pdf.

2 Ibid.

3 Nearly ninety years have passed 'after the US federal law first addressed stock market manipulation'. The principal impetus behind the enactment of U.S. securities law in the midst of the Great Depression was the deterrence of manipulation. Merritt. B. Fox and others, 'Stock Market Manipulation and Its Regulation' (2018) 35(1) Yale J Reg 67, 69.

4 IOSCO, Addendum to IOSCO Report on Investigating and Prosecuting Market Manipulation (April 2013) https://www.iosco.org/library/pubdocs/pdf/IOSCOPD411.pdf.

5 Ibid.

6 On 6 May 2010, flash crash, the leading US stock indices, including the Dow Jones Industrial Average, S&P 500, and Nasdaq Composite Index plunged nearly 10% in a matter of minutes before partially rebounding, wiping out around USD 1 trillion in market value. Tyler Bridegan and Dina Moussa, '*U.S. v. Sarao*: The Flash Crash and A New Effort to Prosecute Market Manipulation and Deceptive Trading Practices' (2017) 1(2) Geo L Tech Rev 396.

7 There is a caveat, though, that official statistics rely on a coarse proxy of regulatory enforcement; the number of reported breaches is likely to be an underestimate of the true total incidents owing to imperfect detection.

statistics released by the European market authority, the incidence of 'suspicious transaction and order reports' (STORs) associated with market manipulation has risen, accompanied by a steady increase in the aggregated number of notifications received by national competent authorities (NCAs) of Member States since 2011.[8] The US and the UK data tell the same stories. The FinCEN suspicious activity report (SAR) published by the US Treasury Department shows that alleged manipulation incidents have increased for a fifth consecutive year from 2016 to 2021, which more than tripled as a result.[9] Similarly, the UK has experienced a spike in manipulation related reports made to the Financial Conduct Authority (FCA): the number of notifications of market manipulation saw a surge, rising from 66 in 2011 to 822 in 2019, even though the numbers dwindled to around 640 after that.[10]

As a result, regulatory intervention aimed at addressing the increased prevalence of market manipulation has been considerably reinforced. In Europe, for example, following the price-rigging (e.g. LIBOR, WMR fix) scandals that broke in the early 2010s, the scope of prohibition has extended to behaviours in relation to benchmarks, and the revised rules have 'accommodated new methods of dissemination of information and other technological changes': all types of media 'as means of communicating misinformation and electronic methods such as algorithmic and high-frequency trading' are now covered by the law.[11] Moreover, 'attempted' manipulation has become subjected to prohibition, regardless of the likelihood or completeness of the potentially manipulative conduct.[12] Meanwhile, subsequent to the disruptive effects of the Flash Crash on securities markets, US regulators have taken the unprecedented step to

---

8 The most recent data covering 2021 and 2022 indicates that 'the majority of notifications covered cases of alleged market manipulation, which accounted for 52% of the total; insider trading make up a lower share in the reference years'. Interestingly, in the period spanning from 2010 to 2018, most STORs received related to insider trading. For details, see European Securities and Markets Authority (ESMA), Report on Suspicious Transaction and Order Reports (STORs) (17 July 2023) https://www.esma.europa.eu/press-news/esma-news/esma-publishes-report-suspicious-transactions-and-order-reports.

9 For the number of filings by types of suspicious activity, refer to SAR filing trending data that is accessible via the FinCEN website https://www.fincen.gov/reports/sar-stats/sar-filings-industry.

10 The number of periodic receipts of STORs, along with their breakdown by types of misconduct and asset classes, is available at the FCA website https://www.fca.org.uk/markets/how-report-suspected-market-abuse-firm-or-trading-venue/number-stors-received-2022.

11 Selina Sagayam, 'New European Market Abuse Regime – What Do Non-EU Incorporated Issuers Need to Know?' *GIBSON DUNN Client Alert* (22 June 2016) https://www.gibsondunn.com/new-european-market-abuse-regime-what-do-non-eu-incorporated-issuers-need-to-know/.

12 Ibid.

enhance transparency and oversight mechanisms, especially for large traders that hold dominant market positions and high-frequency market makers.[13] In addition to imposing certain reporting obligations on covered entities and tighter quoting rules for market makers, market authorities required high-frequency traders to provide 'the details of their strategies as well as their secret computer codes' and introduced a new market-wide trading curb (i.e., circuit breaker).[14]

Nonetheless, various deficiencies are still present. The lack of clarity in legal standards, *inter alia*, generates ambiguity and vagueness in interpretations, thereby impeding consistent and effective law enforcement. There exist differing perspectives on what actually constitutes market manipulation and on what criteria are essential to prove the misconduct, which also varies across jurisdictions.[15] For example, not all jurisdictions require the demonstration or 'proof of intent as a prerequisite for establishing manipulative activity'.[16] Even when intent is a required element to prove manipulation, there are some doubts as to the underlying purpose served by manipulative intent, including inquiries into whether and how it involves the fraudulent misleading of others.[17] Additionally, legal terms and phrases to describe the conduct are arguably 'open and to some extent vague': to give an instance, price manipulation occurs when a price is artificially affected, and an artificial created price as such refers to a price that is subject to manipulation, yet this description corresponds to 'a tautology – only a repetition of the concept'.[18] Applicable law and regulations largely enumerate a non-exhaustive list of indicators of manipulative behaviour with certain examples rather than precisely define the concept, which inevitably complicates our understanding of the nature and scope of market manipulation.

This inquiry provides a critical assessment of the anti-manipulation regime, with a particular focus on the Korean law and regulations. The Korean regime for market manipulation has the aforementioned problem – i.e., a lack of clarity in legal standards of unlawfulness. Moreover, its two-tiered hierarchical

13 Jonathan Spicer, 'FACTBOX: After the flash crash, changes to U.S. markets' *Reuters* (18 February 2011) https://www.reuters.com/article/financial-regulation-flashcrash-idUSN1827676320110218.

14 Ibid.

15 Andri Fannar Bergþórsson, *What is Market Manipulation? An Analysis of the Concept in a European and Nordic Context* in Brill Research Perspectives in International Banking and Securities Law (Brill 2018) 3.

16 IOSCO (n 1) 17–18.

17 Ibid.

18 Bergþórsson (n 15) 4.

system of enforcing the market abuse legislation, which sets it apart from that of other major jurisdictions, exacerbate the problem, rendering the regulatory system overly complex and confusing. Furthermore, the Korean law is silent on algorithmic and high-frequency trading activities that could have potentially manipulative effects on markets.

The rest of this article proceeds as follows. The next section defines the nature and scope of market manipulation, examining the elements that constitute a violation of the rules. Section 3 gives an overview of the regulatory systems in the world's largest and active markets, namely the US, EU, and UK, along with a snapshot of that found in Korean law. Subsequently, the Korean regime for market manipulation is critically reviewed in Section 4, where we analyse in depth the pressing issues surrounding the current legal system and suggests ways in which the regime could be improved. Finally, Section 5 summarises and provides concluding remarks.

2 The Nature and Scope of Market Manipulation

Market manipulation generally refers to any deliberate act which interferes with the free and fair operation of the market, leading to 'an artificial or controlled price' of security prices.[19] The objective of manipulating market prices is to generate profits by capitalising on differentials between a distorted price and its corresponding fair valuation.[20] To this end, traders of interest (i.e., manipulators) engage in securities transactions either individually or in groups, or disseminate false rumours about a stock issue, thereby deceptively inducing other market participants to trade the security. Therefore, market manipulation is commonly blamed for its abusive attributes and often results in both 'criminal and civil (or administrative) liability'.[21]

However, unfortunately, the detection, investigation, and prosecution of such financial misconduct in practice proves to be quite challenging. Despite its regulatory significance, there is 'no satisfactory definition of the term market manipulation', and regulators struggle to discern between illegal price manipulation and legitimate speculative trades.[22] Indeed, current US law

19 James WM. Moore and Frank M. Wiseman, 'Market Manipulation and the Exchange Act' (1934) 2(1) U Chi L Rev 46, 50.

20 IOSCO (n 1) 6.

21 Ibid 5.

22 Daniel R. Fischel and David J. Ross, 'Should the Law Prohibit Manipulation in Financial Markets?' (1991) 105(2) Harv L Rev 503, 506.

does not explicitly define market manipulation, but it rather delineates the parameters of unlawfulness through judicial precedents.[23] By comparison, the EU (and the UK) approach to manipulation offence is more explicit in that the legal system 'proscribes market manipulation by name'.[24] It also aims to offer principle-based guidance that encompasses its various manifestations. Specifically, the European law provides non-exhaustive variants of 'manipulative behaviour, which it derives from the core definitions'.[25] Nonetheless, the provisions are written in broad language, covering any conduct not explicitly mentioned in the statute, with a view to deterring and preventing 'as many forms of manipulations as possible'.[26] This approach comes with a cost: such broad phrasing of rules inevitably lowers legal certainty and predictability for both regulators and market participants.[27]

Additionally, a wide array of perspectives within academic commentary on this subject has created further confusion, and that goes for the judicial interpretations.[28] Admittedly, legal precedents based on fact-specific court decisions have shown 'a lack of uniformity and consistency across cases', and the reliance on an ambiguous 'I know it when I see it' approach has much increased 'uncertainty as to regulatory compliance and enforcement requirements'.[29] It is therefore imperative to clarify the concept of market manipulation so that market authorities map the accurate contours of the misconduct. The ensuing discussion examines that issue in detail.

2.1 *Defining Parameters of Manipulation Offence: Key Legal Standards and Core Elements*

Despite the absence of a universally accepted, clear-cut notion of market manipulation in regulatory statutes, many legal and economic commentators have suggested various explanations for the nature of manipulative trading,

23 Given the lack of a specific and clear definition of the term, it seems atypical for 'a legal prohibition of market manipulation to refer to this practice by its name, instead of merely describing it'. Emilios E. Avgouleas, 'The Mechanics of Market Manipulation' in *The Mechanics and Regulation of Market Abuse: A Legal and Economic Analysis* (Oxford, 2005; online edn, Oxford Academic, 2010) 105–06.

24 Ibid.

25 Rüdiger Veil, 'Market Manipulation' in Rüdiger Veil (ed), *European Capital Markets Law* (3rd edn, Hart 2022) 233.

26 Ibid.

27 Ibid.

28 According to one notable commentator, the law of manipulation 'has become an embarrassment – confusing, contradictory, complex, and unsophisticated'. See Fischel and Ross (n 22).

29 Shaun D. Ledgerwood and Paul R. Carpenter, 'A Framework for the Analysis of Market Manipulation' (2012) 8(1) Rev L & Econ 253, 268.

and have formulated a conceptual framework to determine whether, and if so, to what extent, it should be subject to regulation. Given the literature evidence, one common approach is that any conduct is deemed to be manipulative when it is designed to 'interfere with the free (inter)play of supply and demand in the securities markets'.[30] This formulation has immediate and intuitive appeal since deliberately attempting to influence the supply and demand for a financial instrument can lead to the 'divergence of price from the legitimate market forces'.[31] However, this standard, which focuses on a notion of 'interference', has the same flaw found in earlier treatment of the subject – in all likelihood, manipulative conduct involves interference, and hence logic is 'circular absent a definition of manipulation'.[32]

Another compelling formulation is that market manipulation indicates 'conduct intended to (i) induce people to trade a security, or (ii) force its price to an artificial level'.[33] This theory is an improvement over the one referred to above, in that it explicitly identifies the circumstances that are of particular concern to financial regulators. Indeed, these two criteria delineate the essence of market manipulation, capturing the most salient features of market abuse behaviours. Manipulators can more readily steer market prices in their favourable directions and make profits at the expense of the investing public by inducing other market participants to trade in a stock in question; enticing other investors to trade in a target issue may facilitate creating an artificial price by virtue of the increment of trading pressure. Noteworthy is here that the artificially determined price is defined as 'a price which would be different if the price influencing effort (such as an inducement to trade) were absent'.[34] In this context, the aforementioned elements (i.e., an inducement to trade and creation of an artificial price) are not two distinct types addressed in isolation; rather, they need to be considered in tandem to establish manipulation offence. This is equivalent to saying that one is not sufficient to prove the malfeasance without the other. Without a requirement to identify the inducement of trading, any transactions that cause a price movement, which are common occurrences in markets, may be considered manipulative and consequently penalised, even if they are legitimate. Likewise, deeming a trader's conduct manipulative without assessing its price impact does not make reasonable sense. Without determining the extent to which the market price is affected by

---

30 Fischel and Ross (n 22) 507.

31 IOSCO (n 1) 13.

32 Ibid.

33 Steve Thel, 'The Original Conception of Section 10(b) of the Securities Exchange Act' (1990) 42(2) Stan L Rev 385, 393.

34 Avgouleas (n 23) 110 (citing the classic definition of 'artificial price' offered in the US case of *Great Western Food Distributors* v. *Brannan*, 201 F.2d 476 (7th Cir. 1953)).

the 'suspicious behaviour of the alleged manipulator', any forms of speculation run the risk of being construed as manipulative trading, extending beyond the necessary bounds of prohibition.[35]

However, this approach presents some shortcomings, necessitating a further elaboration of the concept. First, the problem with the element of 'inducement' is that the range of conducts it covers is overbroad; it also includes transactions wherein the involved parties mutually benefit from the trades.[36] If an investor engages in a legitimate transaction, extending a *bona fide* offer to other market participants in good faith, it unquestionably serves as an inducement to trade, yet it should not be deemed as manipulation.[37] Therefore, refining the concept of this element is required. Also, this is why the pivotal role of fraud or deceit is highlighted in conceptualising market manipulation. The rationale for this is straightforward. Investors are typically induced to trade a security in question due to lack of adequate knowledge or information regarding the target issue and prevailing market conditions, and such 'information asymmetry' can be attributable to a manipulator's fraudulent scheme.[38]

Manipulators can make a misrepresentation, that is, 'a false or misleading statement of a material fact of the specific or related investments' with the intent to deceive other market participants.[39] Alternatively, the perpetrators can participate in fictitious transactions, or conceal their genuine intent when executing actual trades.[40] For example, in a wash trade, wherein the same person assumes the roles of both buyer and seller concurrently, thereby creating a false impression of (apparently active) trading activity without incurring any effective change of the beneficial ownership or market risk, the trade 'becomes misinforming' market participants, leading them to be highly susceptible to entering into the transactions.[41] Even if a specific transaction results in a real change in assets held and its entailing risk, it can still deceive other investors as long as the primary motivation behind the order or trade is to affect the value of a financial instrument.[42] Manipulators' trade may send misleading signals to the market in some way, and investors may consequently fall victim to 'concealed attempts' aimed at creating artificial price movements.[43] This may also

35 Ibid 114.
36 Fischel and Ross (n 22) 507.
37 Ibid.
38 Bergþórsson (n 15) 290.
39 Avgouleas (n 23) 117.
40 Ibid.
41 Bergþórsson (n 15) 290.
42 Ibid.
43 Avgouleas (n 23) 116.

be true of manipulators acquiring 'a dominant or controlling position in the market' and exercising market power to 'dictate (or position) the price of the investments concerned to the levels that best suit their interests'.[44] Admittedly, this way of thinking may be counterintuitive – 'the exercise of market power or dominant position relates to' the latter element (price artificiality), not the former one (fraudulent inducement).[45] However, as discussed earlier, these two elements are not mutually exclusive – one does not preclude the existence of the other.[46] Using market controlling power when placing orders or executing trades can exert direct pressure on market prices, but it also has an effect of 'misleading other market participants who see the trades or orders as commercially driven', thereby affecting the value of a target instrument.[47] Noteworthy is here that price alteration stemming from a trading activity (or a mere conception of its potential effect) by itself does not constitute market manipulation, but instead underlying motives driving such transactions and the presence of manipulative intent aimed at conveying the misinformation (or disinformation) to the market via actual trading are likely to be closely scrutinised. This is because the market price is in essence 'a function of the information available', and trading has the potential to influence the market price 'by providing market participants with additional information', regardless of its veracity.[48]

Next, the challenge associated with the element of 'price artificiality' lies in the fact that presenting evidentiary support for it can be quite tricky technically. As mentioned earlier, an artificial price is defined as a price that would deviate from the level in the absence of the 'price influencing efforts', and it is characterised as 'the divergence of price from the legitimate forces of supply and demand'.[49] Rigorous quantification of the price impact of manipulative trading on a target instrument is required to prove this, and, to this end, a statistical method using econometric techniques, commonly referred to as an 'event study', is frequently employed.[50] However, as with every other sophisticated

44 Ibid 148–49.

45 Bergþórsson (n 15) 132.

46 Ibid.

47 Ibid.

48 Fischel and Ross (n 22) 515.

49 Avgouleas (n 23) 110.

50 The premise of this method is that when the market price is found to be 'unexplained by the market model' and is of statistical significance, a causal link 'between the event in question (in this case, market manipulation) and the observed price movements' is established. Min-woo Kang, 'Theories of Causal Nexus in Rule 10b-5 Claims: A Critical Reassessment' (2022) 2(1) L Bus 5, 13.

statistical test, evidencing price distortion using an event study method is susceptible to model risk, rendering it a daunting task.

However, importantly, there is one caveat: not only an 'actual' but also a 'likely effect' on the value of a target falls within the scope of prohibition.[51] It is not contestable that market manipulation has occurred if a fraudulent inducement has had 'an actual effect (*de facto*) on the price of a financial instrument' concerned.[52] Nevertheless, the current anti-manipulation rules stipulate that it suffices for there to be 'a risk of such an effect', even in the absence of demonstrated actual effect on the market prices.[53] This is in effect to alleviate the burden of proof on regulatory authorities, reducing the evidentiary requirements in establishing market manipulation. It is of note that, by the same token, 'attempted' market manipulation is also deemed to be illegal and thus proscribed. Certainly, such broad interpretation and application of the rules is 'intended to make it unnecessary for regulators to prove' that the alleged participation in illegitimate activities actually had manipulative effect.[54]

Taken together, market manipulation is defined as any trading, practices, or conduct deliberately designed to fraudulently induce other investors to enter into a transaction, and likely move the price of a target instrument to an artificial level. To be more specific, materially misinforming factors such as misrepresentations, fictitious transactions, and concealments, act as triggers for market participants to make erroneous decisions, thereby distorting a price formation mechanism.[55] Noteworthy is here that the two core elements introduced herein, namely 'fraudulent inducement' and 'price artificiality', are conceptually interconnected; therefore, they need be considered in conjunction. The proof of one element 'should be tied to the evidencing of' the other element, and this principle is upheld across all major jurisdictions. In particular, in terms of a requirement for showing the existence of a 'fraudulent inducement', a well-established and widely accepted standard posits that a rebuttable presumption arises when a person with 'a substantial, direct pecuniary interest in' securities transactions in question 'takes active steps to effect'

51 Bergþórsson (n 15) 291.
52 Ibid.
53 Ibid.
54 Ibid 257.
55 Material (mis)information is construed in this context as a fact that, based on the perspective of a reasonable investor, is deemed to have 'significantly altered the total mix of information made available'. See Min-woo Kang (n 50) 6 (citing a classic case of *TSC Industries, Inc.* v. *Northway, Inc.*, 426 U.S. 438, 449 (1976)).

a rise or fall in the market prices; i.e., 'a finding of manipulative purpose is *prima facie* established'.[56]

On a related note, cases of manipulation offence are mostly built on circumstantial evidence. They include inference-indicators such as 'the nature of the actions that the behaviour in question consists of (e.g., misrepresentations or artificial transactions)', the direction of other market participants' trade, the gains obtained from the positions, the structure of the manipulative scheme' employed, and others, which are assessed with reference to the trader's commercial needs.[57] Such a heavy reliance on inferences, not direct evidence, may appear somewhat unappealing, but it is 'the most realistic approach in ascertaining manipulative intent, where that is necessary, despite the fact that it is not free from difficulties'.[58] This is because the mental element must be inferred somehow to impose legal sanctions.

2.2 *Forms and Tactics of Market Manipulation*

Market manipulation is not confined to a particular type of trading activity; rather, it can manifest in diverse forms, depending upon the strategies employed. Nevertheless, at the broadest level, market manipulation can be categorised into (i) information-based manipulation and (ii) transaction-based manipulation.[59]

Information-based manipulation involves influencing the price of a target instrument primarily through 'misrepresentations or dissemination of false rumours'.[60] This refers to the communication of misleading information by any means, encompassing: issuers' material misrepresentations, broker-dealers' misstatements, analysts' biased recommendations, and rumours (or fake news) creation on 'social media, as well as on online bulletin boards and in internet chat rooms'.[61] Popular examples of this type of market manipulation include practices such as 'pump and dump' and 'bear raids'. In a pump and

56 *Crane Company* v. *Westinghouse Air Brake Co.*, 419 F.2d 787, 795 (2d Cir. 1969); see also Federal Corp., 25 SEC 227, 230 (1947).

57 Avgouleas (n 23) 117.

58 Ibid.

59 This way of thinking, which distinguishes 'information-based' and 'trade-based' manipulation, originates from a landmark study conducted by two prominent economists. See for details, Franklin Allen and Douglas Gale, 'Stock-Price Manipulation' (1992) 5(3) Rev Financ Stud 503.

60 Bergþórsson (n 15) 84.

61 Securities and Exchange Commission (SEC), 'Updated Investor Alert: Social Media and Investing – Stock Rumours' *Investor Alerts and Bulletins* (5 November 2015) https://www.sec.gov/oiea/investor-alerts-bulletins/ia-rumors.

dump scheme, perpetrators typically 'spread false or misleading information to create a buying frenzy that will pump up the price of a stock and then dump shares of the stock by selling their own shares at the inflated price'.[62] Following the cessation of activities of hyping the stock, the stock price normally falls, resulting in profits for manipulators and losses for other investors. In a bear raid scheme, conversely, a target issue is 'sold short in an effort to drive down the price of the security', which is facilitated by the dissemination of false (or inaccurately negative) information about the target.[63] As other investors sell or short, the price falls and the bear raiders materialises financial gains when covering their short positions.

Transaction-based manipulation requires the 'possibility of giving false or misleading signals as to supply of, demand for or price of financial instruments through an actual order or transaction'.[64] Notably, this manifestation of market manipulation consists of a wide variety of schemes such as 'wash trades', 'matched orders', 'marking the close', 'corner' and 'squeeze' to name a few.[65] Out of these, the first two tactics are classified as fictitious transactions 'aimed at creating a false impression regarding the state' of the market conditions.[66] A wash trade is as previously mentioned; it pertains to transactions wherein the buyer and seller are identical entities, resulting in a lack of genuine change in beneficial ownership or market risk. Matched orders indicate the pairing of 'orders placed by different (but colluding) parties under essentially identical conditions' in terms of price or volume.[67] The rest are not deemed fictitious as they represent genuine trades involving real changes in ownership or exposure to investment risk. Marking the close refers to the practice of 'effecting trades near the close of the trading day in order to influence the closing price'.[68] The resultant price distortion is particularly important, as it often serves as a

62 See the website of the SEC's Office of Investor Education and Advocacy https://www.investor.gov/introduction-investing/investing-basics/glossary/pump-and-dump-schemes.

63 See the SEC, 'Concept Rule: Short Sales' Release Number 34-42037; File Number S7-24-99 (28 October 1999).

64 Veil (n 25) 232.

65 In addition to these, various forms of transaction-based market manipulation exist, encompassing disruptive algorithmic and high-frequency trading practices such as 'layering', 'spoofing', 'momentum ignition', 'ping orders', and others. For a non-exhaustive list of the tactics and their detailed exposition, refer to Annex II section 1 of Commission Delegate Regulation (EU) 2016/522.

66 Avgouleas (n 23) 122.

67 Veil (n 25) 239 (emphasis added in parenthesis).

68 Marcel Kahan, 'Securities Law and the Social Costs of Inaccurate Stock Prices' (1992) 41(5) Duke L J 977, 983.

reference price for the valuation of an asset.[69] In corners and squeezes schemes, a manipulator 'secures a controlling position in the supply of' a target instrument or a related derivative contract. The perpetrator then leverages the dominant position 'to manipulate the price by exploiting investors who need the underlying asset to close out short positions'.[70]

Admittedly, the above classification is arbitrary and is provided solely for the purpose of convenience. Within each category, various forms of manipulation can be further broken down into sub-categories. Besides, manipulators typically 'use a mixture of devices to perpetrate their abusive scheme'.[71] Nonetheless, this categorisation holds some merit as it elucidates the characteristics of each trading strategy and its associated manipulative tactics.

3 Regulatory Frameworks across Jurisdictions

The foregoing analysis suggests that market manipulation is detrimental to the proper functioning of financial markets, 'undermining both the informational and transactional role'.[72] It may introduce to the market not only 'allocative inefficiency' by causing financial instruments to trade at an artificial (or inaccurate) price that 'does not reflect an independent appraisal' of the investments but also 'transactional inefficiency' by rendering market participants to refrain from 'some or all trading (which leads to a reduction in market liquidity) due to the erosion of confidence in the market price as an indicator of true value'.[73] Thus, it is widely accepted that market manipulation should be prohibited to protect market integrity and enhance overall market quality.

Of course, such notion is not without counterarguments. Some commentators contend that it is quite difficult to carry out a profitable manipulation due to liquidity costs and the substantial capital investment required.[74] According to their reasoning, at least 'purely trade-based (as opposed to information-based) manipulation is unlikely to be successful', and the market-wide ban on manipulation may serve as a deterrent, potentially exerting undue influence on

69 Tālis J. Putniņš, 'Market Manipulation: A Survey' (2012) 26(5) Journal of Economic Surveys 952, 956.

70 Ibid.

71 Avgouleas (n 23) 120.

72 Albert S. Kyle and S. Viswanathan, 'How to Define Illegal Price Manipulation' (2008) 98(2) Am Econ Rev 274.

73 Ledgerwood and Carpenter (n 29) 282.

74 For a detailed exposition, see Fischel and Ross (n 22).

even legitimate trading activities.[75] However, it should be noted that a substantial body of theoretical and empirical literature rebuts these claims, revealing the fact that manipulation is rather easily achievable through actual trading.[76] Manipulators purportedly derive profits 'either from pre-existing contracts that are contingent on prices, or by inducing other market participants to trade at manipulated prices'.[77] Against this backdrop, market manipulation largely falls within the prohibitory scope in major jurisdictions (which include the US and the EU), discussed below.

3.1 *The US Legal System and Regulatory Standards*

3.1.1 Law and Regulations Governing Securities Markets

The principal tools for regulating equity market manipulation in the US are Sections 9(a) and 10(b) of the Securities Exchange Act of 1934 ('Exchange Act' or '1934 Act').[78] An array of potential penalties can be levied for violations of the law. The Securities and Exchange Commission (SEC), a market authority, can pursue 'injunctive relief and civil monetary penalties in federal court or through its own administrative procedures'.[79] Criminal sanctions can also be imposed by the Department of Justice (DOJ) for wilful violations of the rules; anyone convicted of a criminal market manipulation offence under the Exchange Act is subject to fines not exceeding USD 5 million, or a prison sentence of up to 20 years, or both; provided that, USD 25 million may be imposed for an entity other than a natural person.[80]

Section 9(a) was formulated to 'prevent rigging of the market and permit operation of the natural law of supply and demand'.[81] Specifically, the statutory provision holds that it is unlawful:

- to enter into wash trades and matched orders, for the purpose of 'creating a false or misleading appearance of active trading' in a security or the market;

75 Putniņš (n 69) 954.

76 For example, manipulators normally hinder market participants from ascertaining the veracity of orders or trades by blending truths and falsehoods in the signal being sent to the markets, and in doing so, they can manipulate a target 'price over a long period of time without losing credibility'. See Ibid 957.

77 Ibid 954.

78 Fox and others (n 3) 114.

79 Rahman Ravelli, 'A Primer on Market Manipulation Regulations in the US and UK' (January 2021) https://www.rahmanravelli.co.uk/assets/Resource-Guides/Market-Manipulation/92edfae54c/Market-Manipulation-Master-Guide-29-Jan-2021.pdf 7.

80 15 USC § 78ff.

81 *United States* v. *Stein*, 456 F.2d 844 (2d Cir. 1972).

- to effect a series of transactions in a security that 'create actual or apparent active trading, or raise or depress prices', for the purpose of 'inducing the purchase or sale of such security by others';
- for broker-dealers and related parties to 'induce the purchase or sale of a security' by spreading information that the security prices will or is likely to move due to market rigging devices;
- for broker-dealers and related parties to knowingly make a material misrepresentation;
- to effect a series of transactions in a security for the purpose of 'pegging, fixing, or stabilising' the prices in violation of the SEC rules and regulations.[82]

There is no controversy over the socially harmful aspects of wash trades and matched orders.[83] By impeding trades that genuinely reflect value assessment by both buyers and sellers, wash or matched trades lead to 'a deviation of the price from its efficient level', and hence impair the price accuracy.[84] It is equally undisputed that the dissemination of false or misleading information with the intent to induce trading in a security has the effect of distorting the decision-making processes of market participants, thereby undermining the proper functioning of a fair and accurate price formation mechanism.

However, when it comes to actual transactions, distinguishing legitimate speculation from illegal manipulation can be quite challenging.[85] This is because open market transactions, in which 'the manipulator has not engaged in any conduct that is inherently or otherwise illegal', may still be deemed as illicit activities, based upon the 'manipulative intent and effect in combination'.[86] Manipulative intent (or purpose) is a subject element to constitute an offence, and it is typically inferred from circumstantial evidence.[87] On a related note, courts and regulators have demonstrated willingness to find a violation of Section 9(a) when a transaction is associated with external interests held by the perpetrator. It has been accepted by the SEC that 'an external interest creates an evidential presumption', thereby establishing a *prima facie*

---

82 15 USC § 78i(a).

83 Fox and others (n 3) 115.

84 Ibid.

85 The term 'transactions' herein includes 'not only completed purchases or sales but also bids and orders to purchase or sell securities'. See *SEC* v. *Lek Sec. Corp.*, 276 F. Supp. 3d 49, 62 (S.D.N.Y. 2017); *SEC* v. *Malenfant*, 784 F. Supp. 141, 145 (S.D.N.Y. 1992).

86 Maxwell K. Multer, 'Open-Market Manipulation Under SEC Rule 10b-5 and its Analogues: Inappropriate Distinctions, Judicial Disagreement and Case Study: FERC's Anti-Manipulation Rule', (2011) 39(2) SEC REG LJ 97.

87 Fox and others (n 3) 116.

case.[88] Courts have also taken the same position, acknowledging that 'the purpose of profiting from a price change pursuant to an external interest is at least a form of manipulative purpose'.[89]

Meanwhile, it is worth noting that while pegging or fixing the price is prohibited because of its distorting effects, there are instances where such activity is allowed, particularly when the SEC deems it 'necessary or appropriate in the public interest or for the protection of investors'. Relatedly, Regulation M states that the permit for stabilising activities is exceptionally considered to 'prevent or retard a decline in the market price of a security in connection with an offering'.[90]

Next, Section 10(b) is another major source of authority for regulating market manipulation. The statutory provision outlaws manipulative practices, specifically prohibiting the use of 'any manipulative or deceptive device or contrivance in connection with the purchase or sale of any security, in contravention of' the SEC rules and regulations.[91] The general anti-fraud regulation, Rule 10b-5 is such a rule promulgated thereunder. With a view to refining the prohibition outlined in Section 10(b), the Commission rule makes it unlawful:
- to employ any device, scheme, or artifice to defraud;
- to make any untrue statement of a material fact or to omit to state a material fact necessary in order to make the statements made, in the light of the circumstances under which they were made, not misleading;
- to engage in any act, practice, or course of business which operates or would operate as a fraud or deceit upon any person, in connection with the purchase or sale of any security.[92]

To establish manipulation claim for damages under Rule 10b-5, a plaintiff must show: '(i) manipulative acts; (ii) damages; (iii) reliance; (iv) scienter; (v) in connection with the purchase or sale of securities; (vi) furthered by the defendant's use of the mails or any facility of a national securities exchange'.[93] In a government action for manipulation under Rule 10b-5, however, it is presumed that a demonstration of two of these elements – damages and reliance – would not be required.[94]

88 Ibid.

89 Ibid 117 (citing *Crane* v. *Westinghouse Air Brake Co.*).

90 17 CFR § 242.104.

91 15 USC § 78j(b).

92 17 CFR § 240.10b-5.

93 *La. Pac. Corp.* v. *Merrill Lynch & Co.*, 571 F. App'x 8 (2d Cir. 2014) (citing *ATSI Communications, Inc.* v. *Shaar Fund, Ltd.*, 493 F.3d 87 (2d Cir. 2007)).

94 *SEC* v. *Kelly*, 765 F. Supp. 2d 301 (S.D.N.Y. 2011).

Important here is that Section 10(b) and Rule 10b-5 are loosely worded and broadly phrased, aiming at proscribing financial misconduct in a general sense rather than specifically targeting market manipulation.[95] Such flexible and versatile nature of the anti-fraud clauses has directed the legal discourse on market manipulation primarily toward examining the circumstances in which manipulative behaviours would contravene Section 10(b) and Rule 10b-5, rather than Section 9(a).[96] In actuality, the historical precedents indicate that Section 9(a) has 'played only a minimal role in the development of manipulation jurisprudence in securities law, despite the obvious relevance of its language'.[97]

Also, there are other reasons that have contributed to such developments in case law. Until 2010, Section 9(a) applied merely to cases 'involving exchange-traded securities', thereby excluding most instances of manipulative trading that occur outside its regulatory perimeter, particularly those more likely to involve 'thinly traded over-the-counter issues'.[98] Furthermore, there was some courts' perception that Section 9(a)'s intent to induce element has 'a distinct and more specific' nature than Rule 10b-5's scienter requirement, and thus 'creates a higher burden of proof for the plaintiff than that borne under Rule 10b-5'.[99] But the 'pre-2010 limitations on Section 9(a)'s reach' do not now exist – its coverage extends to any securities not registered.[100] Also, there appears to be minimal benefit in differentiating between scienter, which signifies 'a mental state embracing intent to deceive, manipulate, or defraud', and a (fraudulent) inducement to trade.[101] In other words, there are no significant barriers for Section 9(a) claims anymore. Therefore, the continued prevalence of claims for market manipulation under Section 10(b) and Rule 10b-5, not under Section 9(a), appears to be attributed to 'path dependency'.[102]

Nonetheless, it is also true that challenging a specific behaviour as manipulation under the general anti-fraud regulations has posed a conundrum for

---

95 This represents the legislative intent of the legislature; Section 10(b) was designed as 'a catchall clause' to uphold the integrity of securities markets, ensuring investor protection 'against manipulation of stock prices' and containing 'dishonest practices of the market place'. *Basic, Inc.* v. *Levinson*, 485 U.S. 224, 230 (1988); see also *Chiarella* v. *United States*, 445 U.S. 222, 226 (1980).

96 Fox and others (n 3) 118.

97 Ibid 117.

98 Ibid.

99 See *Chemetron Corp.* v. *Business Funds, Inc.*, 682 F.2d 1149, 1162 (5th Cir. 1982).

100 Fox and others (n 3) 123.

101 *SEC* v. *Competitive Techs., Inc.*, No. CIV.A.3:04CV1331 (JCH), 2005 WL 1719725, at *7 n. 7 (D. Conn. 21 July 2005).

102 Fox and others (n 3) 123.

jurisprudence, creating significant confusion for both regulators and market participants. This is primarily due to the Supreme Court's narrow interpretation of the statutory provision, which has emphasised the significance of 'deceit and misrepresentation in a Section 10(b) claim, almost transforming Section 10(b) into a statute that only caught fraud and fraud-like claims within its ambit'.[103] It has left lower courts with the question of whether any facially legitimate transactions *per se* (i.e., open market transactions) 'could even by itself constitute illegal manipulation', and a sharp split in authority has naturally followed.[104]

For example, the Third Circuit ruled that actual trading alone cannot be considered a manipulation offence without an accompanying additional unlawful act, stating that 'the essential element of the (manipulation) claim is that inaccurate information is being injected into the market'.[105] In the court's view, a legitimate transaction does not convey 'inaccurate' information to the market, and therefore, does not meet the criteria for fraudulent or deceptive conduct. However, the D.C. Circuit opposed to this theory. The court of appeals acknowledged that an open market transaction on its own may be unlawful under Rule 10b-5, asserting that 'manipulation can be deemed illegal solely based on the actor's intent'.[106] In a more recent decision, importantly, the Second Circuit adopted a similar stance. It held that 'in a manipulation claim, a showing of reliance may be based on *market activity* intended to mislead investors by sending a false pricing signal to the market, upon which victims of the manipulation rely'.[107] This ruling stands in stark contrast to the Third Circuit's opinion, as it accepted the SEC's argument that 'the essence of manipulation is not a misrepresentation, but market activity – the buying and selling of shares – that itself creates a false pricing signal'.[108] Today, unfortunately, the issue of confusion and disparities of judicial outcomes stemming from the current circuit split remains unsettled and continues unabated. Although lower courts seem to favour the reasoning of the Second Circuit over

103 Ibid 118. See, for example, *Schreiber* v. *Burlington Northern*, 472 U.S. 1, 8 n. 6 (1985); *Santa Fe Industries, Inc.* v. *Green*, 430 U.S. 462, 476 (1977); *Ernst & Ernst* v. *Hochfelder*, 425 U.S. 185, 199 (1976).

104 Ibid 119.

105 *GFL Advantage Fund, Ltd.* v. *Colkitt*, 272 F.3d 189, 205 (3d Cir. 2001).

106 *Markowski* v. *SEC*, 274 F.3d 525, 529 (D.C. Cir. 2001).

107 *Fezzani* v. *Bear, Stearns & Co.*, 777 F.3d 566, 571–72 (2d Cir. 2015).

108 Ibid.

that of the Third Circuit, the Supreme Court has not yet offered clarity on the matter and remains silent.[109]

Meanwhile, although its utility is relatively limited, Section 17(a) of the Securities Act of 1933 is pertinent to the discussion, particularly in relation to the offering of securities in primary markets. Its structure and phrasing bear resemblance to that of Section 10(b) of the Exchange Act. However, of note is that its scope of regulation is 'broader because civil claims by the SEC under Section 17(a) may be based on negligent conduct, while such claims under Section 10(b) require proof of scienter'.[110] By comparison, the potential sanctions for violations of Section 17(a) are less severe; any person convicted of a wilful violation is liable to fines of up to USD 10,000 or imprisoned not more than five years, or both.[111]

3.1.2 Law and Regulations Governing Commodities and Derivatives Markets

Manipulation occurs not only in securities markets but also in commodities or any related derivatives markets, with key statutory and regulatory requirements found in Sections 4(c), 6(c), and 9(a) of the Commodity Exchange Act (CEA). The CEA was formulated with a view to 'protecting the innocent individual investor – who may know little about the intricacies and complexities of the commodities market – from being misled or deceived'.[112] Taking into account the fact that trading and pricing commodities or related derivatives contracts are 'susceptible to excessive speculation and can be manipulated, controlled, cornered or squeezed', in particular, a set of anti-manipulations rules has been hitherto implemented.[113] A knowing violation of the rules amounts to 'a felony punishable' by a fine of up to USD 1 million or imprisonment not exceeding 10 years, or both.[114]

Section 4(c)(a) of the CEA stipulates that it is unlawful to engage in any commodities derivative transaction that is 'of the character of, or is commonly known to the trade as, a wash sale or accommodation trade, or is a fictitious sale', and further states that any transaction that is 'used to cause any price

109 Fox and others (n 3) 122. A petition seeking a review of the law on open market manipulation was submitted to the Supreme Court, but the highest court denied petition for writ of certiorari (*Koch* v. *SEC*, U.S., No. 15-781, 3/28/16).

110 See Rahman Ravelli (n 79) 18.

111 15 USC § 77x.

112 *Loginovskaya* v. *Batratchenko*, 764 F.3d 266, 270 (2d Cir. 2014).

113 Jerry W. Markham, *Law Enforcement and the History of Financial Market Manipulation* (Routledge 2015) 90.

114 7 USC § 13(a).

to be reported, registered, or recorded that is not a true and *bona fide* price' falls within the scope of the statutory ban.[115] Section 6(c)(3) makes it illegal for 'any person, directly or indirectly, to manipulate or attempt to manipulate the price of any swap, or of any commodity in interstate commerce, or for future delivery on or subject to the rules of any registered entity'.[116] Section 9(a)(2) sets forth similar provisions deeming it illegitimate activities for 'any person to manipulate or attempt to manipulate the price of any commodity', or 'to corner or attempt to corner any such commodity'.[117]

The legal prohibitions require proving the following elements: (i) the manipulator 'possessed the ability to influence prices; (ii) specifically intended to execute manipulative scheme; (iii) an artificial price existed; (iv) the accused caused the artificial price'.[118] When pertaining to the case of 'attempted' price manipulation, of course, showing the existence of 'an artificial price' is not required – establishing only that the alleged manipulator 'acted (or failed to act) with the purpose or conscious object of causing or effecting a price or price trend in the market that did not reflect the legitimate forces of supply and demand' is necessary.[119] That said, this a bit lenient standard does not imply that 'a mere intent to affect prices is enough'; rather, it underscores the necessity of demonstrating a specific intent to create artificial price.[120]

However, providing evidence for the elements above can be easier said than done, and, among other things, establishing 'price artificiality' proves to be technically very tricky. Indeed, the historical record shows that the market authority (in this case, the Commodity Futures Trading Commission (CFTC)) has encountered significant troubles bringing enforcement actions under the existing legal provisions: 'in fact, in 35 years, there has been only one successful prosecution for manipulations'.[121] For this reason, during the global financial crisis, there was a widespread political consensus regarding the need for the CFTC to possess the enhanced capacity to prosecute and prevent fraud scandals in commodity and derivatives markets effectively.

Against this backdrop, on 21 July 2010, the Dodd-Frank Wall Street Reform and Consumer Protection Act (popularly known as the 'Dodd-Frank Act')

115 7 USC § 6c(a).
116 7 USC § 9(3).
117 7 USC § 13(a)(2).
118 *Frey* v. *CFTC*, 931 F.2d 1171, 1175 (7th Cir. 1991); see also *In re Soybean Futures Litigation*, 892 F. Supp. 1025 (N.D. Ill. 1995).
119 *CFTC* v. *Donald R. Wilson & DRW Invs., LLC*, No. 13 Civ. 7884 (RJS) (S.D.N.Y. Nov. 30, 2018).
120 Ibid.
121 CFTC, Remarks of Commissioner Bart Chilton to Metals Market Investors, Washington, D.C. (23 March 2010) https://www.cftc.gov/PressRoom/SpeechesTestimony/opachilton-30.

became the law, which introduced some notable provisions to reinforce the anti-manipulation rules. This includes, *inter alia*, a new provision of Section 6(c)(1) that has incorporated the notion of 'fraud and deceit' into the CEA pursuant to Section 753 of the Dodd-Frank Act. Specifically, Section 6(c)(1) of the CEA makes it 'unlawful for any person, directly or indirectly, to use or employ, or attempt to use or employ, in connection with any swap, or a contract of sale of any commodity in interstate commerce, or for future delivery on or subject to the rules of any registered entity, any *manipulative* or *deceptive* device or contrivance, in contravention of' the CFTC rules and regulations.[122] Obviously, the language of this new provision mirrors that of Section 10(b) of the Exchange Act, empowering the CFTC to exercise anti-manipulation authorities equivalent to those of the SEC.[123] In actuality, to refine Section 6(c)(1) prohibitions, the CFTC 'issued an analogous to Rule 10b-5, Rule 180.1', in which the federal agency has determined that it is illegal 'for any person to *intentionally* or *recklessly* use or employ, or attempt to use or employ, any manipulative device, scheme, or artifice to defraud'.[124]

With *de facto* equivalent rules in place, both the SEC and the CFTC can share case precedents when enforcing the rules.[125] Particularly noteworthy is here that there was the extension of the scienter standard in Rule 180.1 cases, where it now incorporates 'recklessness' as well as 'manipulative intent'. This is the outcome of addressing the criticism that the CFTC's existing 'specific intent' standard of proof has been harder to enforce than the fraud-based 'reckless conduct' standard employed by other agencies such as the SEC.[126] While the Supreme Court has not yet settled the 'question whether recklessness suffices to fulfil the scienter requirement', lower courts have construed scienter to encompass 'either actual intent to defraud or recklessness'.[127]

To be sure, this amendment to the CEA and the CFTC regulations marked a significant step towards 'expanding the reach of the CFTC to prohibit manipulative and fraudulent behaviour'; it lowered the legal hurdle considerably 'by

---

122 7 USC § 9(1).

123 Rahman Ravelli (n 79) 25.

124 Ibid (citing 17 CFR § 180.1(1)).

125 Ledgerwood and Carpenter (n 29) 258.

126 See Press Release: Federal Regulators Finalise Tough New Market Manipulation Rule Required by Cantwell (7 July 2011) https://www.cantwell.senate.gov/news/press-releases/federal-regulators-finalize-tough-new-market-manipulation-rule-required-by-cantwell.

127 *Matrixx Initiatives, Inc. v. Siracusano*, 563 U.S. 27 (2011); see also *Tellabs, Inc. v. Makor Issues & Rights, Ltd.*, 551 U.S. 308 (2007).

eliminating the requirement to show an artificial price and lowering the scienter standard to recklessness for fraud-based manipulation'.[128]

3.2 *The EU/UK Legal Systems and Regulatory Standards*

3.2.1 The EU Law and Regulations

In Europe, the Union-wide legislation, the Directive 2003/6/EC (Market Abuse Directive (MAD)) was the principal tool that prohibited market manipulation, which has the overarching goal of safeguarding 'the reliability and accuracy of price formation'.[129] The current EU regime, consisting of a Regulation (EU) 596/2014 on market abuse (MAR) and a Directive 2014/57/EU on criminal sanctions for market abuse (CSMAD), has further reinforced the legal system by both expanding the scope of regulation and 'providing greater deterrence through stricter sanctions'.[130] For reference, the EU regulation (MAR) is itself 'legally binding and directly applicable', whereas the directive (CSMAD) 'requires transposition by Member States'.[131]

The EU MAR has introduced more harmonised administrative rules or sanctions for any (natural or legal) person found guilty of the offence, including a maximum penalty of 'at least three times the amount of the profits gained, or losses avoided', and a maximum fine of 'at least EUR 5 million for natural person' and not less than 'EUR 15 million or 15% of total annual turnover for legal person'.[132] The civil market abuse regime also sets out other administrative measures it imposes on a perpetrator: 'an order requiring the person responsible for the infringement to cease the conduct, the disgorgement of the profits gained or losses avoided due to the infringement, withdrawal or suspension of the authorisation' and others.[133] Furthermore, the EU law allows for Member States to have additional sanctioning powers and 'provide for higher levels of punishments than those referred to' in MAR.[134]

As an extra component of the EU regulation, CSMAD has been established to 'work with MAR to create a stronger market abuse regulatory framework with

128 CFTC, 'Fact Sheet: Anti-Manipulation and Anti-Fraud Final Rules' (14 July 2011) https://www.cftc.gov/sites/default/files/idc/groups/public/@newsroom/documents/file/amaf_factsheet_final.pdf.

129 Veil (n 25) 229.

130 Ibid.

131 Sébastien Bagot, 'A new European Framework: MAR and CSMAD' (9 November 2016) https://ec.europa.eu/assets/agri/market-sectors/cereals/commodity-expert-group/2016-11-09/dgfisma-bagot-overview-new-eu-legal-framework.pdf.

132 Art 30(2) Regulation (EU) 596/2014.

133 Ibid.

134 Art 30(3) Regulation (EU) 596/2014.

harmonised (criminal) sanctions throughout the EU', reflecting the fact that criminal punishments can have a greater deterrent effect.[135] The CSMAD sets forth minimum standards for criminal penalties, including 'maximum term of imprisonment of at least 4 years' for natural persons who are engaged in illegal market manipulation, and for legal persons, fines with 'other sanctions such as exclusion from entitlement to public benefits or aid, temporary or permanent disqualification from the practice of commercial activities, placing under judicial supervision, judicial winding-up'.[136] As already mentioned, however, these standards are only the minimum requirements, and it thus 'remains open to each EU country to go beyond the requirements' of the criminal regime.[137]

The key anti-manipulation rules are specified in Articles 12 and 15 of the MAR: Article 15 expressly prohibits a person from 'engaging in or attempting to engage in market manipulation', and Article 12 delineates the concept of market manipulation, coupled with 'practically relevant examples of these core definitions'.[138] In addition, Annex I of the MAR offers a 'non-exhaustive list of indicators that could be taken into account when investigating' the unlawful conduct.[139] Specifically, Article 12(1) of the MAR makes it offence to do the following activities:

- entering into a transaction, placing an order to trade or any other behaviour which (i) gives, or is likely to give, false or misleading signals as to the supply of, demand for, or price of, a financial instrument, (ii) or secures, or is likely to secure, the price thereof at an abnormal or artificial level;
- entering into a transaction, placing an order to trade or any other activity or behaviour which affects or is likely to affect the price of one or several financial instruments, which employs a fictitious device or any other form of deception or contrivance;
- disseminating false or misleading information through the media, including the internet, or by any other means, including the spread of rumours,

---

135 Niel Robson, 'The CSMAD: significant imminent changes to EU market abuse and insider dealing rules' *Financier Worldwide Expert Briefing* (May 2015) https://www.financierworldwide.com/the-csmad-significant-imminent-changes-to-eu-market-abuse-and-insider-dealing-rules.

136 Art 7 to 9 Directive 2014/57/EU. This Directive is compliant with the requirement laid down in Article 83(2) of the Treaty on the Functioning of the European Union (EU Treaty), which stipulates that 'if the approximation of criminal laws and regulations of the Member States proves essential to ensure the effective implementation of a Union policy ..., directives may establish minimum rules with regard to the definition of criminal offences and sanctions in the area concerned'.

137 Niel Robson (n 135).

138 Veil (n 25) 229.

139 Ibid 232.

where the person who made the dissemination knew, or ought to have known, that the information was false or misleading;
- transmitting false or misleading information or providing such inputs in relation to a benchmark where the person who made the transmission or provided the input knew or ought to have known that it was false or misleading, or any other behaviour which manipulates the calculation of a benchmark.[140]

According to the form classification previously outlined, the first type of misconduct aligns with transaction-based manipulation, whilst the third one is associated with information-based manipulation. The second form of manipulation highlights the role of fraud and deceit, 'serving as a catch-all clause'.[141] The final one, benchmark manipulation, is new and was introduced in the wake of the LIBOR scandal which came to light in 2012; given its critical 'importance in providing reference prices for financial instruments or contracts', there was a strong call for stringent prohibitions on benchmark manipulation at both the international and European levels.[142]

Notably, the EU law takes a step further in defining market manipulation, providing more specific types of manipulative trading. Per Article 12(2), the following behaviours are, *inter alia*, considered as market manipulation:
- securing a dominant position over the supply of or demand for a financial instrument, which has, or is likely to have, the effect of fixing, directly or indirectly, purchase or sale prices or creates, or is likely to create, other unfair trading conditions;
- buying or selling of financial instruments, at the opening or closing of the market, which has or is likely to have the effect of misleading investors acting on the basis of the prices displayed;
- placing orders to a trading venue, including any cancellation or modification thereof, by any available means of trading, including by electronic means, such as algorithmic and high-frequency trading strategies and which has a manipulative effect by;
  (i) disrupting or delaying the functioning of the trading system of the trading venue or being likely to do so;

140 Art 12(1)(a) to (d) Regulation (EU) 596/2014.

141 Veil (n 25) 241.

142 Eckhard Binder, 'Review of the Benchmark Regulation: to address the phasing-out of the London Interbank Offered Rate (LIBOR) index' *European Parliamentary Research Service Briefing* (October 2020) https://www.europarl.europa.eu/RegData/etudes/BRIE/2020/654187/EPRS_BRI(2020)654187_EN.pdf.

(ii) making it more difficult for other persons to identify genuine orders on the trading system of the trading venue or being likely to do so, including by entering orders which result in the overloading or destabilisation of the order book; or

(iii) creating or being likely to create a false or misleading signal about the supply of, or demand for, or price of, a financial instrument, in particular by entering orders to initiate or exacerbate a trend;

- taking advantage of occasional or regular access to the traditional or electronic media by voicing an opinion about a financial instrument while having previously taken positions on that financial instrument and profiting subsequently from the impact of the opinions voiced on the price of that instrument, without having simultaneously disclosed that conflict of interest to the public;
- buying or selling on the secondary market of emission allowances or related derivatives prior to the auction held with the effect of fixing the auction clearing price for the auctioned products at an abnormal or artificial level or misleading bidders bidding in the auctions.[143]

While not exhaustive, these guidelines offer both market participants and regulators valuable albeit incomplete tools for analysing transactions or trade orders, particularly when considered alongside the indicators outlined in Annex I of the MAR. As referred above, Annex I enumerates indicators pertaining to manipulative behaviours.[144] First, when investigating suspicious conduct relating to false or misleading signals as to the supply and demand for a financial instrument (Article 12(1)(a) offence), market authorities are likely to monitor the following factors, among other things:

- the extent to which orders to trade given or transactions undertaken represent a significant proportion of the daily volume of transactions in the relevant financial instrument, in particular when those activities lead to a significant change in their prices;
- the extent to which orders to trade given or transactions undertaken by persons with a significant buying or selling position in a financial instrument;
- whether transactions undertaken lead to no change in beneficial ownership of a financial instrument;
- the extent to which orders to trade given or transactions undertaken or orders cancelled include position reversals in a short period and represent a significant proportion of the daily volume of transactions in the relevant financial instrument;

143 Art 12(2)(a) to (d) Regulation (EU) 596/2014.

144 Art 12(3) Regulation (EU) 596/2014.

- the extent to which orders to trade given or transactions undertaken are concentrated within a short time span in the trading session and lead to a price change which is subsequently reversed;
- the extent to which orders to trade given change the representation of the best bid or offer prices in a financial instrument and are removed before they are executed; and
- the extent to which orders to trade are given or transactions are undertaken at or around a specific time when reference prices, settlement prices and valuations are calculated and lead to price changes which have an effect on such prices and valuations.[145]

Next, when it comes to the employment of a fictitious device or any other form of deception or contrivance (Article 12(1)(b) offence), the following questions are likely to be addressed by market authorities:

- whether orders to trade given or transactions undertaken by persons are preceded or followed by dissemination of false or misleading information by the same persons or by persons linked to them; and
- whether orders to trade are given or transactions are undertaken by persons before or after the same persons or persons linked to them produce or disseminate investment recommendations which are erroneous, biased, or demonstrably influenced by material interest.[146]

Indeed, all these traits encompass various aspects of manipulative trading discussed earlier. However, it is worth noting that the indicators by themselves do not permit an automatic inference that the alleged behaviour qualifies as market manipulation. To be found guilty of a violation of the law, regulators must be able to demonstrate that the respective behaviour in question meets the condition set out in Article 12(1) and (2) of the MAR, all things considered.

The EU law also provides for certain exceptions to the aforementioned rules. Article 12(1)(a) of the MAR provides a clause of proviso stating that market manipulation could not be deemed to have occurred, provided that 'the person entering into a transaction, placing an order to trade or engaging in any other behaviour establishes that such transaction, order or behaviour have been carried out for legitimate reasons, and conform with an accepted market practice' established by a competent authority.[147] This entails a 'reversal of the burden of proof'; that is, a defendant, who is the perpetrator, is required to demonstrate that her transactions or trade orders are based on legitimate grounds and are adhere to market practices deemed adequate by national

145 Annex I § A(a) to (g) Regulation (EU) 596/2014.

146 Annex I § B(a), (b) Regulation (EU) 596/2014.

147 Art 12(1)(a) Regulation (EU) 596/2014.

supervisory authorities.[148] On a related note, the MAR provides that 'accepted market practices means a specific market practice that is accepted by a competent authority in accordance with Article 13' (Article 3(9)), and Article 13 sets out the criteria that regulators may take into account in determining an acceptable market practice.[149] The criteria herein encompass factors such as the impact of the relevant practice on market quality (which includes transparency, liquidity, and efficiency), as well as the 'structural attributes of the relevant market, such as the types of financial instruments traded and the composition of market participants, including the extent of retail-investor participation'.[150]

Further, the MAR explicitly provides exemptions for certain trades from the prohibitive measures of the market manipulation regulations. Under Article 5 of the MAR, 'trading in own shares in buy-back programmes' and 'trading in securities or associated instruments for the stabilisation of securities' are not prohibited, provided that they comply with the requirements and conditions set out in the MAR and the applicable regulatory technical standards.[151] In essence, these transactions align with the concept of market manipulation, as they involve the issuer or financial institutions steering the market and resulting in the price at artificial level. However, the legislature and regulators acknowledge the significance of such transactions in operating a firm's ordinary business activities, and thus permit them exceptionally.

In order to benefit from the safe harbour rules, the trades must be carried out in accordance with adequate disclosure obligations and trading conditions. For buy-back programmes, 'the full details of the programme' must be disclosed before the commencement of trading, and the issuer is required to report trades 'to the competent authority of the trading venue and subsequently disclose to the public'.[152] Moreover, although exemptions are allowed for the trades, the MAR ensures that the issuer's purchasing own shares does 'not lead to an artificial price increase by higher acquisition prices or shortage of shares on the free market'.[153] The EU law therefore imposes 'adequate limits on price and volume'; the issuer is prohibited from 'purchasing shares at a

148 Veil (n 25) 240.

149 Ibid 241.

150 Art 13(2)(a) to (g) Regulation (EU) 596/2014. For further specifications of these criteria, see Commission Delegated Regulation (EU) 2016/908.

151 The detailed regulatory technical standards for the conditions applicable to buy-back programmes and stabilisation measure are specified in Commission Delegated Regulation (EU) 2016/1052.

152 Art 5(1)(a), (b) Regulation (EU) 596/2014.

153 Veil (n 25) 247.

price higher than the highest price of the last independent trade and bid' on the corresponding trading venue, and issuers may 'not purchase on any trading day more than 25% of the average daily volume of the shares on the trading venue'.[154] Likewise, financial institutions engaged in stabilisation activities (i.e., credit institutions and investment firms) are subject to a number of restrictions. As with buy-back programmes, the MAR requires the adequate public disclosure and reporting to the competent authority both prior to and after implementing stabilisation measures.[155] Additionally, stabilisation activities may be legitimately exempted from the MAR prohibition, only when they are undertaken 'in the context of a significant distribution of securities exclusively for supporting the market price of those securities for a predetermined period of time, due to a selling pressure in such securities'.[156] Noteworthy is here that such trading 'must have an immediate relation to an offering'; hence, in the case of an initial offer, the stabilisation period 'starts on the date of commencement of trading and ends no later than 30 calendar days thereafter', and in the case of a secondary offer, the limited period 'starts on the date of adequate public disclosure of the final price of the securities and ends no later than 30 calendar days after the date of allotment'.[157]

Overall, it is evident that the EU market manipulation regulations are more comprehensive and specific compared to those stipulated by the US law. The statutory provisions offer detailed explanations on definitive features of market manipulation and a number of instances thereof. Of course, there remains some ambiguity and uncertainty in several aspects of the EU rules. For example, it is questionable whether 'concealing information contrary to existing legal obligations' constitutes market manipulation, because the EU law does 'not explicitly provide for such an offence'.[158] Additionally, it is unclear whether 'the civil law liability for damages of manipulators' is recognised by the EU legislature; the MAR is silent on that issue, and there is a sharp split among court rulings in Member States concerning whether private enforcement should be allowed[159] Nevertheless, it appears that there are no significant regulatory gaps

154 Art 5(1)(c) Regulation (EU) 596/2014. See also Art 3(2), (3) Commission Delegated Regulation (EU) 2016/1052.

155 Art 6(1) to (4) Commission Delegated Regulation (EU) 2016/1052.

156 Art 3(2)(d) Regulation (EU) 596/2014.

157 Veil (n 25) 249. See also Art 5(1)(a), (b) Commission Delegated Regulation (EU) 2016/1052.

158 Ibid 235.

159 Ibid 255. Indeed, a noteworthy disparity in court judgments is evident between Germany and other Member States. As opposed to other jurisdictions (including Austria, France, Greece, Italy and Portugal) that recognise the civil law liability, the German courts rejected the 'possibility for private enforcement', contending that the prohibition on market

identified thus far, owing to the extension of the material scope of application of the prohibitions' and the incorporation of the broadly phrased regulatory standards.[160]

3.2.2 The UK Law and Regulations

The UK operates anti-manipulation regulations under its own MAR as 'incorporated into UK domestic law through only minor amendments made to the Financial Services and Markets Act 2000 (FSMA) and the Financial Services Act 2012 (FSA)'.[161] Indeed, the EU-style law is hitherto applicable in the UK to a large extent: upon the UK's departure from the EU, the EU legislation that 'applied directly in the UK at the point of exit was transferred onto the UK statute by the European Union (Withdrawal) Act 2018' which is commonly referred to as retained EU law (REUL).[162] Administrative, civil or criminal sanctions may be imposed for breaches of the rules.[163] The market authority, the FCA, can impose 'a (civil) penalty of such amount as it considers appropriate on the person who has contravened Article 15 of the MAR or publish a statement censuring' the perpetrator pursuant to the provision of Section 123 of the FSMA.[164] The authority can also secure the High Court judgement awarding injunction restraining the wrongful acts.[165]

Under Sections 92 of the FSA, an offender can also be penalised criminally: any person who is found 'guilty of an offence is liable, on conviction on indictment, to imprisonment for a term not exceeding 10 years or a fine, or both'.[166] According to the Section 89 of the FSA, a person breaches the rule if she 'makes the statement or conceals the facts with the intention of inducing, or is reckless as to whether making it or concealing them may induce' other

manipulation primarily serves to uphold the 'functioning of the market at a macro-level', rather than prioritise investor protection. For a more detailed discussion on private enforcement within the EU and national legal systems, see Vassilios D. Tountopoulos, 'Market Abuse and Private Enforcement' (2014) 11(3) Eur Co Financial Law Rev 297.

160 Veil (n 25) 256.

161 Rahman Ravelli (n 79) 35.

162 HM Treasury, Policy statement – Building a smarter financial services framework for the UK (December 2022) https://assets.publishing.service.gov.uk/media/6391d6128fa8f53bac58e476/Building_a_smarter_financial_services_framework_for_the_UK_.pdf 9.

163 Notably, as opposed to the Regulation (EU) 596/2014, the Directive 2014/57/EU (CSMAD) was not incorporated in the UK law, and hence criminal penalties, specifically applicable to market abuse behaviours, are addressed within the UK national laws such as the Financial Services Act 2012 (FSA) or the Fraud Act 2006 (FA).

164 See § 123(1) to (3) FSMA.

165 § 381 FSMA.

166 § 92(1)(b) FSA. Criminal fines, as with civil monetary penalties, lack a predetermined cap.

investors to trade in a target instrument.[167] The offence is committed as well, per Section 90, when a perpetrator 'intends to create a false or misleading impression as to the market in or the price or value of any relevant investments', and intends, by creating such impression, either to '(i) induce another person to acquire, dispose of, subscribe for or underwrite the investments or to refrain from doing so', or to '(ii) make a profit for herself or cause loss to another or to be aware that it is likely to produce that result'.[168] Fraud Act 2006 is another tool to punish manipulators by criminal sanctions. A person is in breach of the anti-manipulation rules in accordance to Section 2 of the Fraud Act 2006 if she 'dishonestly makes a false (untrue or misleading) representation, and intends, by making the representation, to make a gain or to cause loss to another or to expose another to a risk of loss'.[169] A Section 2 violation is subject to the same penalties as those prescribed for the FSA offence, where 'upon conviction on indictment, a perpetrator may face imprisonment for a maximum term of 10 years, a fine, or both'.[170]

It should be however noted that the UK regime is currently in the process of repealing the retained EU law and of replacing it with the new UK-specific financial legislation.[171] This includes the market abuse regime, which governs illegal market manipulation.[172] In a number of areas, reforms to update and refine the regulatory system are being undertaken, but the exact timetable is still to be set. With anticipated legislative changes poised to have a profound effect on anti-manipulation regulations, much will hinge on how they ultimately proceed.

---

167 § 89(1), (2) FSA.

168 § 90(1) to (4) FSA.

169 § 2(1) Fraud Act. In the Supreme Court's opinion, the alleged act would be considered 'dishonest by the lay objective standards of ordinary reasonable and honest people'. See *Ivey* v *Genting Casinos (UK) Ltd t/a Crockfords* [2017] UKSC 67.

170 § 1(3) Fraud Act.

171 As of this writing, the Retained EU Law (Revocation and Reform) Act 2023 that intends to 'strip REUL of any special legal status and any EU interpretive features at the end of 2023' passed and took effect on 1 January 2024. As a result, retained EU law supremacy has been abolished and the retained law (now referred to as 'assimilated law') no longer need to be interpreted in line with general principles of the EU law. However, the government's stance is to 'phase the revocations over time to ensure orderly transition'. Expectedly, it will take some years to complete the process of the repealing or amending existing EU law provisions and ultimately to construct the new UK regulatory framework. See Erza Zahabi and others, 'Beginning of the End of EU Law in the UK?' *Akin Insights: Alerts* (13 July 2023) https://www.akingump.com/a/web/n7bAeiFLoMkGKhT77MSi3w/7Z7Dez/beginning-of-the-end-of-eu-law-in-the-uk-v4.pdf.

172 Schedule 1 of FSMA 2023 sets forth that it revokes the Regulation (EU) 596/2014 by the end of 2023.

3.3 *The Korean Legal System and Regulatory Standards*

3.3.1 The Traditional Approach to Prohibitions on Market Manipulation

The Korean regime for market manipulation dates back to 1962, when the former Securities and Exchange Act (증권거래법) was first established. At present, the Financial Investment Services and Capital Markets Act (자본시장과 금융투자업에 관한 법률), which is commonly called the Capital Markets Act or FSCMA, enacted in 2007 to supersede the Securities and Exchange Act delineates all pertinent rules of market manipulation offences.

The key regulatory provisions targeting market manipulation are found in Article 176 to 178 of the FSCMA. All these provisions have been, in fact, implemented with the benefit of hindsight vis-à-vis US and European regulatory reforms; they are thus similar to those prescribed by the US and EU laws. Article 176 of the FSCMA, which is a core provision, was formulated with reference to Section 9(a) of the US Exchange Act.[173] Specifically, it prohibits any person from doing the following activities:

- to engage in wash trades or matched orders with the intent to create a false or misleading appearance of active trading in listed securities or exchange-traded derivatives, or to mislead other investors into making the wrong decisions;
- to give a false or misleading impression of active trading in listed securities or exchange-traded derivatives, or to enter into transactions which influence the price of them, for the purpose of inducing the purchase or sale of such instruments by others;
- to disseminate a rumour that the prices of listed securities or exchange-traded derivatives in question are being under the influence of the manipulators' trades, or to make a false or misleading representation of material facts in trading such instruments, for the purpose of inducing the purchase or sale of them by others;
- to effect a series of transactions for the purpose of fixing or stabilising the price of the listed securities or exchange-traded derivatives: provided that such measures shall not apply to the cases that meet safe harbour requirements (e.g., stabilisation of securities or market creation);

173 The legislative history indicates that this provision was formulated with reference to Article 159 of the Japanese Financial Instruments and Exchange Act (金融商品取引法), which, in turn, draw inspiration from the Section 9(a) of the US Exchange Act. Jung Soo Lee, 'A Research on a Stock Manipulation through Actual Trading: Interpretational Approach and Complementary Measures to the Act' (2020) 33(1) Commer Case Law 167, 190.

- to engage in conduct that drives a fluctuation in, or secures the price of financial instruments, in case where any of securities, derivatives, or underlying assets thereof are listed on an exchange, in connection with the purchase or sale of such instruments or other transactions with intent to earn or cause another to earn illicit profits from the trade.[174]

Article 178 is another provision that can be used to prohibit manipulative behaviours. This regulation is referred to as 'a general anti-fraud rule' in the Korean Capital Markets Act, encompassing a catch-all clause that broadly defines financial misconduct as follows:

- in connection with purchase or sale of and other transactions of financial instruments, it is unlawful (i) to use an unfair means, scheme, or trick, (ii) to make a false or misleading representation or omission of material facts, (iii) to use an inaccurate market price with intent to induce others to trade;
- it is prohibited to disseminate a rumour, use a deceptive scheme, or make a threat with the intent to trade or make other transactions in financial instruments or attempt to influence the market prices.[175]

This provision bears a significant resemblance to the US SEC Rule 10b-5, with only minor alteration in wordings.[176] Hence, it is well accepted that Article 178 serves to enhance the prohibitions delineated in other market abuse regulations, addressing the potential regulatory voids; that is, in terms of market manipulation offences, it is designed to supplement Article 176 referred to above.[177]

Indeed, Article 178 significantly expands the scope of instruments and activities covered by the law. The scope is no longer limited to listed securities or exchange-trades derivatives but it also applies to all types of financial instruments irrespective of the trading venue. Furthermore, as a general anti-fraud clause, Article 178(1)1 has extended the regulatory perimeter to include the abstract notion of acts such as the use of an 'unfair' means, scheme or trick. Regarding the question of what precisely constitutes the use of unfair means, considerable controversy has arisen among legal scholars and practitioners. In particular, the inquiry focused on whether or how the concept of 'unfair' differs that of 'fraud' as defined by the US SEC Rule 10b-5. Relatedly, the Supreme

174 Art 176(1) to (4) FSCMA.

175 Art 178(1), (2) FSCMA.

176 The legislative history indicates that this provision was formulated with reference to Article 157 and 158 of the Japanese Financial Instruments and Exchange Act (金融商品取引法), which, in turn, draw inspiration from the US SEC Rule 10b-5. See Im Chool Park, 'A Study on Unfair Transactions under Article 178 of the Financial Investment Services and Capital Markets Act' (2013) 14(2) Korean J Secur Law 353, 365.

177 Ibid 369.

Court of Korea interpreted it so broadly, holding that the term an 'unfair' means under Article 178(1)1 of the FSCMA refers to any means considered 'wrongful' according to the societal conventions.[178] However, in a subsequent decision, the highest court suggested a more clearly defined criterion for what constitutes an unfair means. According to the Court's opinion, the notion of unfairness (in connection with trading financial instruments) should be assessed by considering (i) whether the act in question is prohibited by law, (ii) whether it undermines fair competition and misleads investors into making wrong decisions, and (iii) whether it poses a risk to the fairness, credibility, and efficiency of capital markets.[179]

The severe penalties of the Korean law are imposed on the person who commits the offence of the rules. Under Article 443 of the FSCMA, any person found guilty of a criminal offence, engaging in manipulative behaviour in contravention of Article 176 or 178, is subject to punishment, including 'imprisonment for at least 1 year or a fine equivalent to three to five times the profit accrued or loss avoided by the violation'.[180] Furthermore, with the most recent amendment to the Act in 2023, the regulatory authority (namely, the FSC) is now empowered to impose 'a penalty surcharge equivalent to two times the profit gained or loss avoided by the violation' on the perpetrator: provided that, in cases where 'no profit was gained or loss avoided by the violation, or where it is impracticable to calculate such profit or loss', the upper limit of the administrative fine will be KRW 4 billion.[181] However, in the event of a criminal fine being imposed for the same violation, the administrative surcharge may be rescinded entirely, or a portion equivalent to the criminal fine may be deducted from it.[182]

---

178 Supreme Court Decision 2011Do8109 Decided 27 October 2011.

179 Supreme Court Decision 2013Do9933 Decided 16 January 2014. Following this precedent, subsequent rulings have taken the position that certain forms of fraud and deception are necessary as a criterion for determining the unfairness of acts. See also Supreme Court Decision 2014Do6910 Decided 30 March 2017; Supreme Court Decision 2013Do6962 Decided 12 April 2018; Seoul Southern District Court Decision 2018Godan3255 Decided 10 April 2019.

180 Art 443(1)4 to 9 FSCMA. However, in cases where no profit or loss occurs, or it is 'impractical to calculate such profit or loss, or when the amount equivalent to five times the profit gained or loss avoided by the violation does not exceed KRW 500 million', the criminal fine will be not more than KRW 500 million. In addition, when 'gains accrued or losses avoided by a violation exceed KRW 500 million, a punishment by imprisonment will be aggravated' as follows: (i) if the profit or loss amounts to at least KRW 5 billion, the perpetrator may face imprisonment for a period ranging from 5 years to life; (ii) if the profit or loss amounts to at least KRW 500 million but does not exceed KRW 5 billion, the minimum term of imprisonment is 3 years.

181 Art 429-2(1) FSCMA.

182 Art 429-2(2) FSCMA.

Meanwhile, the Korean law allows for private enforcement. Article 177 of the FSCMA recognises civil liability for damages caused by a manipulator's violation of the rules outlined in Article 176, provided that the right to claim damages ceases by prescription unless it is exercised 'within 2 years from the point at which the claimant becomes aware of a violation' of the rules, or 'within 5 years from the time such violation was committed'.[183]

3.3.2 A More Recent Innovative Legislation: Prohibitions on Market Disturbances

As per above, the perpetrators who breach the market manipulation regulations can be subject to stringent criminal sanctions. However, we know too well that in a criminal proceeding, the onus is upon the prosecution to establish, 'beyond any reasonable doubt', the culpability of the defendant.[184] Under a key principle of criminal law, *nulla poena sine lege* (no penalty without a law), enforcement authorities bear a substantial burden of proof, which presents challenges in efficiently and effectively policing financial misconduct.[185] In particular, showing the existence of manipulative intent or purpose often proves to be quite difficult without a confession from the accused manipulator. In actuality, numerous cases have ended in acquittals due to the failure to establish the existence of these subjective elements.[186]

Against this backdrop, the Korean legislator and the government introduced a new provision, Article 178-2, into the FSCMA in 2014.[187] In doing so, they aimed to fill the regulatory gap and protect investors more broadly by prohibiting misconduct that could potentially undermine market integrity, albeit to a lesser extent than the abusive behaviours referred to above.[188] Specifically, in terms of market manipulation, Article 178-2(2) makes it unlawful to 'engage

183 Art 177(1), (2) FSCMA.

184 Criminal facts must be 'proved to the extent that there is no reasonable doubt' pursuant to Article 307(2) of the Criminal Procedure Act (형사소송법).

185 Jung Soo Lee, 'A Research on the Direction of Legislative Improvement for the Market Abuse Rule' (2023) 24(1) Korean J Secur Law 93, 98.

186 Ibid 101 (citing Seoul High Court Decision 2014No465 Decided 30 May 2014; Seoul Southern District Court Decision 2016Kohap437 Decided 19 January 2018).

187 The new provision then came into effect in July 2015. In fact, it prohibits improper trading practices, encompassing market abuse behaviours related not only to market manipulation but also to insider trading which involves trading with material non-public information. However, regulations concerning insider trading are beyond the scope of this inquiry.

188 Financial Services Commission (FSC), Press Release: the Cabinet passed a partial amendment of the Financial Investment Services and Capital Markets Act to prohibit market disturbances (23 December 2014).

in any of the following acts in connection with the trade, etc. of any listed securities or exchange-traded derivatives':

- An act that adversely affects, or is likely to, adversely affect the market price by massively submitting asking prices at which orders are unlikely to be filled, or by repeatedly correcting or cancelling the quotes after their submission;
- An act that adversely affects, or is likely to, adversely affect the market price through the execution of a fictitious trade, having no intention of transferring the rights thereof;
- An act that adversely affects, or is likely to, adversely affect the market price by conducting a trade after conspiring in advance with a third party to purchase the same instruments, at the same price or at an agreed value at the same time, for the purpose of a profit or loss transfer or tax evasion;
- An act that is likely to give a false or misleading impression on the status of supply and demand for the instruments or the prices, or is likely to distort market prices, by spreading a rumour, devising an artifice, and others.[189]

It should be however noted that this does not apply in case where the act in question is covered by either Article 176 or 178. Moreover, this rule differs from existing market abuse regulations in that it encompasses activities that are 'likely to have an impact' (as well as have 'actual impact') on the market price. Notably, unlike the aforementioned market abuse rules, Article 178-2(2) does not require the presence of manipulative intent (or purpose) aimed at inducing others to engage in transactions (see Figure 1 below). With the reduction in the burden of proof, the corresponding level of punishment is relatively diminished. A wrongdoer is only punishable by a penalty surcharge, not a criminal fine; the government may 'impose a penalty surcharge not exceeding KRW 500 million on a person who violates Article 178-2'.[190] As maybe easily guessed by now, this regulation was formulated with reference to the EU MAR. By virtue of broadening the scope of prohibitions and mitigating the burden of proof, the roles and responsibilities of the market authority have increased considerably. However, it is also true that the legal status as an independent sanctioning measure is somewhat precarious in relation to other market abuse rules and institutional arrangements for its remit, discussed below, creating

189 Art 178-2(2) FSCMA.

190 Art 429-2(4) FSCMA. However, in case where the amount equivalent to 1.5 times the profit (including unrealised gains) obtained from a trade, or the loss avoided due to the violation, exceeds KRW 500 million, a penalty surcharge not surpassing 1.5 times the profit amount or avoided loss may be imposed.

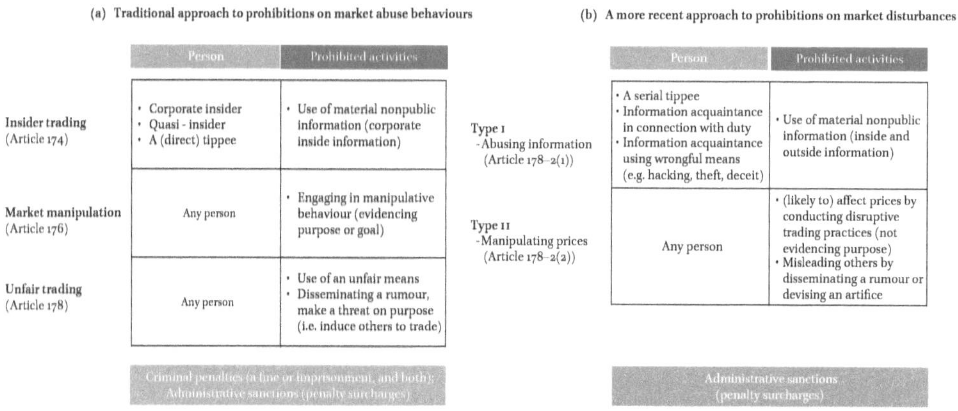

FIGURE 1 Dual-track system for market abuse offences in Korea
SOURCE: FINANCIAL SERVICES COMMISSION

much uncertainty and compromising its effectiveness as a deterrent to financial misconduct.

4 Issues Analysis and Suggestions for Improvement

4.1 *A Need to Revise the Rules Based on Well-established Legal Standards*

The foregoing discussion of the Korean anti-manipulation regime highlights its alignment with the systems of the US and EU financial law. Further, the regulatory system even appears to be robust and comprehensive. However, unfortunately, the reality is not like what it seems. As clearly seen in the previous section (see Section 3.3), the statutory provisions do not expressly define the elements required to establish the financial misconduct; rather, they only enumerate the possible forms of manipulative behaviour. Moreover, the Korean market manipulation law overlooks the need to contain the risk of manipulative effect and to prevent manipulative attempts. Also, importantly, it mainly targets instruments traded on regulated markets (i.e., listed securities or exchange-traded derivatives), which is too narrow in scope. This is mainly due to the rules being developed through ad-hoc adjustments to changes in market circumstances, rather than being formulated based on well-defined regulatory principles. Indeed, the Korean law has opted to mirror legal and regulatory instruments found in other major jurisdictions without offering proper contextual explanation or guidance. However, this approach can result in the formulation of market abuse rules being predominantly left to court decisions, potentially adding to complexity and confusion for both regulators and market participants. Of particular significance is it for countries, such as Korea adhering to the civil law tradition, where emphasis is placed on legal codes crafted by the legislature. Therefore, we call for the need to revise the rules on well-established legal standards, stressing that statutory provisions, not judge-made laws, should serve as the primary source of guidance in determining what constitutes market manipulation.

To this end, first off, the law should clearly and explicitly define the misinformation requirement for market manipulation offences. As fully discussed in Section 2.1, market manipulation requires a showing of the presence of an 'inducement' to trade and the creation of 'price artificiality' to establish its unlawfulness. In particular, the former element (i.e., inducement) plays a central role in differentiating manipulative trades and legitimate transactions. In essence, inducing others to trade implies that a manipulator alters the investment decisions of other market participants in some way, irrespective of whether it occurs through the dissemination of false or misleading information or through engaging in fictitious or actual transactions. To put it another way, but for such manipulative efforts, it is presumed that there would be no distortion in the decision-making processes of other investors, nor in the price formation mechanism. Noteworthy is here that inducing others to trade in a financial instrument is not an illegal practice *per se*; the critical factor lies in its fraudulent nature.[191] What matters most is that a manipulator sends a false or misleading signal or provide such an input to the market. It becomes more problematic when the perpetrator deliberately intends to mislead market participants by either knowingly misstating (or lying about) the material facts or orchestrating trading conditions that do not reflect a natural consequence of the interplay of supply and demand in the markets, all with an 'ulterior motive' for influencing the value of a target instrument.[192] In this respect, it can be argued that misinformation is a vital criterion in determining manipulative intent or purpose.[193]

191 Arguably, implicit in the specific intent requirement is the notion that deception is a key determinant of manipulation by trading. Inducing other market participants to trade is equivalent to deceiving those investors into 'believing that the manipulator's purchases or sales are a *bona fide* expression of supply and demand in the market, rather than the creation of a price mirage'. See Norman S. Poser, 'Stock Market Manipulation and Corporate Control Transactions' (1986) 40(3) U Miami L Rev 671, 704.

192 Bergþórsson (n 15) 290.

193 This argument is consistent with that made by professor Andri Fannar Bergþórsson, who claimed that 'misinformation is an essential element of all types of market manipulation'. See Ibid.

Second, the law should give greater consideration to the risk of manipulative effect (i.e., a likely effect on the value). As earlier seen in the EU regulation (see Section 3.2.1), establishing an element other than an inducement, namely the price artificiality, does not necessarily require the presence of a price movement caused by manipulative efforts. Instead, it suffices to consider the likelihood of such an effect, regardless of whether there is an actual price impact on the market.[194] However, the Korean securities law deals with the requirements in two separate provisions (i.e., Article of 176 and 178-2), prioritising regulatory scrutiny based on the actual effect over the potential influence on the market prices. Put simply, in case where there is a proven impact on the price of a target instrument, Article 176 is invoked, leading to potential criminal sanctions for the offender. On the contrary, if the influence on value is deemed probable, Article 178-2 applies, resulting in the imposition of administrative sanctions (or penalty surcharges), not criminal penalties. However, there is no good reason to decouple a 'likely effect' from an 'actual effect' on the market price driven by manipulative trading and to treat them as completely different factors. Indeed, taking into account the fact that an artificial price movement is typically inferenced from circumstantial evidence, there is no real benefit to drawing a line between them.[195]

Third, the law should include prohibitions against attempting to engage in market manipulation. Deterring and preventing manipulative attempts is reasonable and justifiable for prophylactic purposes, and for the very reason, the US and EU law explicitly ban attempts to manipulate market prices. However, Article 176 of the FSCMA, the very heart of the Korean market manipulation law, does not mention anything about regulating attempted market manipulation. Relatedly, a counterargument could be made that Article 178(2) makes it offence to 'disseminate a rumour, use a deceptive scheme, or make a threat' with an attempt to affect the market prices. Nevertheless, given that the introduction of Article 178 as a general anti-fraud provision into the FSCMA is intended to supplement and complement the existing market abuse rules, Article 178 is not construed to supersede or override Article 176.[196] Hence, this signifies a regulatory void that requires special attention from the Korean legislature and government.

Fourth, in relation to Article 176(2) that sets forth the rules concerning market manipulation caused by actual trading, the subparagraphs addressing the

194 Ibid 291–292.

195 Notably, an event study, a commonly used method for estimating the impact of price manipulation, also yields a mere statistical inference.

196 Park (n 176) 377 (citing Supreme Court Decision 2011Do8109 Decided 27 October 2011).

dissemination of a rumour or misrepresentation of a material fact (i.e., 176(2)2 and 176(2)3) are deemed redundant as well as erroneously located within this provision. Instead, they could be more efficiently and effectively regulated under Article 178(1)2 and 178(2), which stipulates the prohibitions against the *de facto* same conduct referred to above.[197] Thus, it may be advisable to remove these two clauses when revising the law.

Last but not least, the law should expand the scope of current prohibitions from listed securities or exchange-traded derivatives contracts to all types of financial instruments. The principal reason why the Korean market manipulation legislation narrowly focuses on instruments on regulated markets is, as mentioned earlier, due to its reference to Section 9(a) of the US Exchange Act, which, until 2010, was 'only applicable to alleged manipulations involving exchange-traded securities'.[198] However, 'the ambit of section 9(a) is now wide', extending its reach to any securities not registered.[199] Likewise, there is no such restriction in European law; in current MAR regime, market manipulation rules apply to any financial instruments not only traded on regulated markets but also traded over the counter (OTC) markets.[200] Further, as evidenced by the 2013 amendment to Article 176(4) of the FSCMA, Korean law has broadened its coverage of regulation to securities, derivatives, or their underlying assets, to the extent that any of these instruments are listed on an exchange. Thus, there is no need to limit the regulatory scope to certain instruments any more. Importantly, all types of financial instruments are required to fall within the regulatory perimeter.

Taken together, a viable change to the current market manipulation law provisions (specifically, Article 176 of the FSCMA) is outlined as follows:

(1) it shall be unlawful for any person to engage in a transaction, place an order to trade, or conduct any other activity which gives, or is likely to give, a false or misleading signal, or an impression as to the supply of, demand for, or price of any financial instruments, for the purpose of inducing the purchase or sale of such instruments by others, and is likely to affect their value, if such person knows, or recklessly disregards, that such behaviour is false or misleading and likely to affect the value of financial instruments;

197 The severity and extent of criminal punishment for breaches of Articles 176 and 178 is also identical pursuant to Article 443. See Lee (n 173) 195–197.

198 Fox and others (n 3) 117.

199 Ibid 123.

200 Veil (n 25) 231.

(2) it shall be unlawful for any person to disseminate information by any means, which gives, or is likely to give, false or misleading signals, or an impression as to the supply of, demand for, or price of any financial instruments, for the purpose of inducing the purchase or sale of such instruments by others, and is likely to affect their value, if such person knows, or recklessly disregards, that such information is false or misleading and likely to affect the value of financial instruments;
(3) it shall be unlawful for any person whose behaviour would violate subparagraph (1) and (2), to attempt such misconduct;

where 'false or misleading' signals indicate any activities which are not perceived to be *bona fide* in connection with the purchase or sale of financial instruments. For purposes of this provision, such activities shall, *inter alia*, may include but not limited to the following:

(i) wash trades or matched orders;
(ii) a significant trading volume of financial instruments occurring at the opening or closing of the market;
(iii) securing a dominant position over the supply of or demand for a financial instrument;
(iv) placing large trade orders at prices unlikely to be executed, and subsequently revising or cancelling the quotes repeatedly after their submission;
(v) opining about a financial instrument, while having previously taken positions on that financial instrument, without simultaneously disclosing the conflict of interest to the public in a proper and effective manner.

This proposal represents just one of several potential options aimed at enhancing the Korean market manipulation regime, and is therefore neither definitive nor conclusive. However, the Korean legislature and government may find it worth considering as a workable solution.

4.2 *A Need to Reform the Current 'Two-Tiered' Hierarchical Enforcement System*

At enforcement level, as aforementioned, the Korean law has split the market abuse regime into a two-tiered hierarchical system. That is, while the regulatory framework operates a sanctions regime wherein criminal or administrative proceedings for market abuse can be brought, the principle of 'criminal punishment first' is applied. Indeed, until very recently, 'sanctions applicable to the traditional types of market abuse behaviours (i.e., insider trading, market manipulation, and unfair trading) and a relatively new class of malpractices (i.e., market disturbance) have been mutually exclusive', and the enforcement system has heavily relied on criminal punishment rather than on civil

TABLE 1 The adjudication of market abuse cases over the past 5 years (2017–2021)

Infringements	Traditional market abuse behaviour (insider trading/market manipulation/unfair trading)		Market disturbance	Total
Actions	Accuse to/charge with the prosecution	Accuse to the prosecution and administrative sanctions	Penalty surcharges (civil penalties)	
The accused (persons)	1,006	22	47	1,075
Proportion (%)	93.6	2.0	4.4	100.0

Note: Administrative sanctions include disciplinary measures, such as suspension of duties, requests for dismissal, and institutional warnings, as well as fines imposed on regulated entities.
SOURCE: FINANCIAL SERVICES COMMISSION

or administrative penalties.[201] Table 1 below confirms this fact, demonstrating that more than 90 percent of purported instances of market abuse have been referred to the prosecution service for the commencement of criminal proceedings, leaving only a small fraction of the remaining cases within the purview of independent handling by market authorities.[202]

This pecking order system has long been under criticism, particularly in terms of effectiveness of its enforcement tools in deterring financial misconduct.[203] Among others, such a heavy reliance on criminal punishments to combat the versatile nature of market abuse has been recognised as a key obstacle to effectively penalising wrongdoers and seeking the disgorgement of ill-gotten profits. As Figure 2 displays, the judicial process typically requires a prolonged period, averaging 2–3 years, to reach conclusions and finalise cases, thereby posing challenges to the timely enforcement of penalties against

201 Min-woo Kang, 'Enforcing the market abuse regime in Korea: recent developments and challenges ahead' (2021) 16(4) Cap Mark Law J 528, 530.

202 FSC, Press Release: Measures to Strengthen Capacity to Respond to Unfair Trade Practices in Capital Markets (28 September 2022).

203 FSC, Press Release: Implementation of the Comprehensive Measures to Eradicate Illegal Activities for the Sound Development of the Securities Market (19 October 2020).

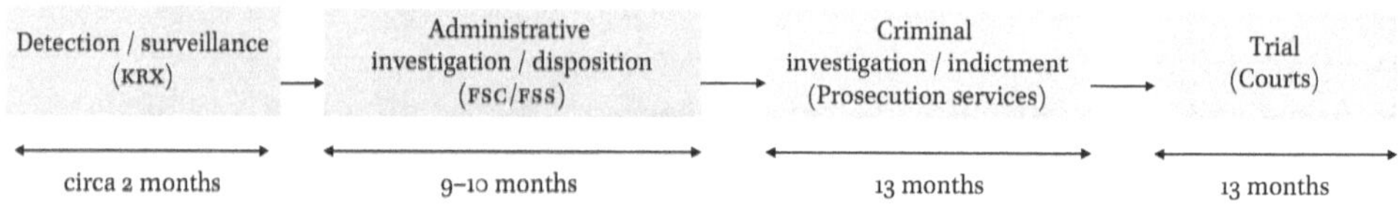

FIGURE 2 The duration for processing of market abuse cases in Korea
SOURCE: FINANCIAL SERVICES COMMISSION

offenders.[204] Moreover, public prosecutors often struggle to establish evidence of the accused's illicit activities due to the strict burden of proof required for finding criminal liability. As a result, the success rate of indictment by the criminal authority has remained suboptimal, registering below 50 percent, and many of them were 'given only minor penalties, such as probation, even if they are indicted'.[205]

It should also be noted that such a two-tiered hierarchical system carries the inherent risk of creating regulatory voids. Consider the following hypothetical scenario. In a market manipulation case, regulators, relying on indirect or circumstantial evidence, determine that the actions of a perpetrator meet the criteria for an offence punishable under criminal law, which is punishable by imprisonment or criminal fines. Consequently, they refer the case to the Prosecution Service. However, prosecutors, after criminal investigation, are unable to find the accused person's guilt beyond a reasonable doubt and are hesitant to pursue an indictment. In such circumstance, the alleged wrongdoer may not only avoid criminal sanctions but also evade administrative penalties. This is because of the fact that under the current 'dual-track' enforcement system, once a case is deemed a criminal offence, it cannot be considered concurrently in administrative proceedings; namely, distinct *corpus delicti* are applicable to criminal and civil market abuse rules, respectively.[206]

---

204 FSC, Press Release: Measures to Strengthen Capacity to Respond to Unfair Trade Practices in Capital Markets (28 September 2022). See also Political Affairs Committee, *A Draft on Partially Amended Financial Investment Services and Capital Markets Act* (Bill No 2122985, June 2023).

205 Kang (n 201) 531. Reportedly, over the past five years (from 2016 to 2020), only 44.2% of cases filed by the market authority with prosecutors resulted in criminal charges. Additionally, based on the 2020 rulings of the Korean Supreme Court, 40.6% of such indicted persons were granted probation.

206 On a related note, unfair or unjust situations may arise that while a perpetrator who has committed a relatively minor offence is subject to penalty surcharges, the accused who is deemed to have committed a more serious crime may evade even administrative sanctions if prosecutors fail to establish the requisite criminal elements. Indeed, a recent court ruling in Korea directly tackled this issue and conducted a comprehensive

In this respect, the most recent amendment to the FSCMA (which became a law on 18 July 2023 and entered into force on 19 January 2024) is truly a significant step forward, in that it has empowered the market authority (in this case, the FSC) to impose penalty surcharges on perpetrators found liable for all types of market abuse offences. By virtue of the rules newly established by Article 429-2 of the FSCMA, financial regulators are now able to impose administrative monetary penalties on any person who is in violation of Article 174 (insider trading), 176 (market manipulation), and 178 (unfair trading), as well as the existing Article 178-2 (market disturbance). As a consequence, any person accused of breaching the market abuse rules may be subjected to both criminal and administrative penalties for the same facts, which was not feasible under the previous enforcement regime.

That being said, this newly implemented enforcement system is of limited utility, as it continues to put some constraints on the ability of financial regulators to exercise their authority to impose administrative penalties on lawbreakers. To be specific, although Article 429-2(1) authorises the FSC's levy on penalty surcharges as an extra regulatory toolkit, Article 380(1) of the Enforcement Decree thereunder stipulates that, in principle, the FSC may impose administrative penalties on perpetrators who have violated market abuse regulation (i.e., infringed Article 174, 176, and 178 of the FSCMA) only after the market authority has been notified of the results of a criminal investigation from the prosecutor general. To be sure, this restriction presents a significant hurdle to timely and efficient sanctioning offenders; as demonstrated above, it usually takes over one year for prosecutors to complete their investigation and decide whether to indict the suspect or not. Of course, there is a proviso allowing the FSC to impose penalty surcharges on an offender at its discretion, if and only if (i) it has already consulted with the prosecutor general and agreed on the matter, or (ii) it has not been informed of the results of a criminal investigation even after one year passed since the alleged case was referred to the prosecutor service (see Figure 3 below). However, even this safe harbour provision does not apply in case where there is a valid reason for the delay in confirming the investigation results, such as deferred prosecution (or suspension of the indictment), or where imposing administrative penalties in advance may conflict with the findings of the criminal investigation.

Eventually, notwithstanding the recent reform of the enforcement regime, the longstanding principle of 'criminal punishment first' has remained largely

analysis of the pertinent considerations. See Seoul High Court Decision 2020Nu63940 Decided 13 April 2022. See also the Supreme Court Decision 2021Du50215 Decided 1 February 2022, which cited the original trial decision.

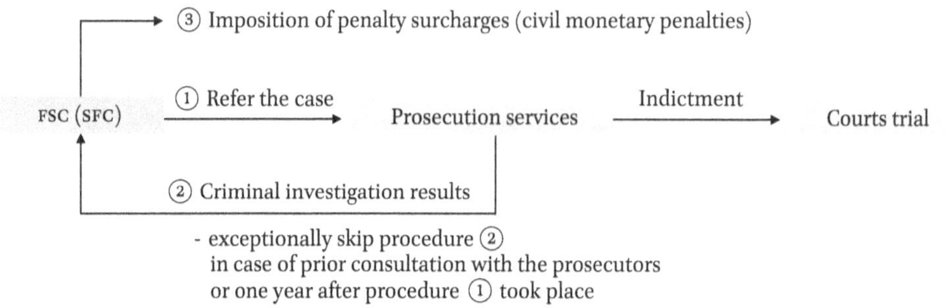

FIGURE 3 The procedural framework for taking enforcement action against market abuse offences in Korea
SOURCE: FINANCIAL SERVICES COMMISSION

unchanged. Civil or administrative penalties continue to be subordinate to criminal sanctions, primarily considered as supplementary or complementary measures. By the same token, they are unlikely to be utilised conclusively and independently. Indeed, scepticism has arisen regarding whether the recent shift in sanctions regime will truly bring about significant changes in securities law enforcement in Korea.[207]

Thus, this situation calls for a more fundamental change of the sanctions system for market abuse in Korea. Specifically, the sanctioning practice of prioritising criminal punishments for market abuse offences must be rejected. While turning to rigorous criminal and judicial proceedings offers certain benefits, such as addressing due process concerns and ensuring procedural fairness, adhering strictly to the 'criminal punishments first' principle is not a panacea. This approach results in a loss of impetus for reform 'by maintaining the status quo'.[208] The Korean lawmakers and government should admit that enforcing the market abuse rules 'through administrative sanctions, *inter alia*, civil monetary penalties, can streamline procedures for the imposition of punishment, thereby enhancing the efficiency and effectiveness of the sanctions regime'.[209] And more importantly, they must acknowledge the fact that 'market authorities are better placed than courts to enforce regulations when knowledge and experience on how markets work are required'.[210] Accordingly, Article 429-2 needs further revision; the recently crafted provision

207 For a relevant discussion on this issue, see Kang (n 201) 532.
208 Ibid 535.
209 Ibid 533.
210 Andrea Perrone, 'EU Market Abuse Regulation: The Puzzle of Enforcement' (2020) 21(2) Eur Bus Organ L Rev 379, 386.

is required to remove conditional stipulations that limit financial regulators' authority to impose sanctions. Further, as a consequence of the reform, the current Article 178-2 can be safely repealed, since the statutory provision has now become redundant.[211]

Nevertheless, there still remain some critical issues concerning the proposed regime outlined above. Among other things, as the new market abuse rule now allows both criminal and administrative proceedings for the same facts, it must be able to clearly and explicitly delineate the legal standards distinguishing between criminal and non-criminal offences. Relatedly, it is noteworthy that in a market manipulation case, the Korean Supreme Court determined that the term 'manipulative purpose' refers to any intent to induce others to trade a security 'by misleading them into believing that the observed market price reflects the natural interplay of supply and demand for the instrument'. Further, the highest court highlighted that the presence of any other purposes, regardless of their significance, is not important, and it 'suffices to establish an element of recklessness'.[212] However, we know too well that criminal and non-criminal (civil or administrative) sanctions serve distinct punitive and educative purposes as well as effects to align behaviours with social norms, respectively, and therefore require different constituent elements.[213] In this context, it would be imperative for any new legislation to expressly set forth the two different mental elements (or the states of mind) for criminal (requiring wilfulness or bad faith) and administrative enforcement (based on recklessness). In addition, the precedents and related case law developments regarding Article 178-2 of the FSCMA accumulated thus far could provide some useful guiding principles for establishing the legal standards.

Another legal issue surrounding the new enforcement system pertains to the 'due process' concern. Admittedly, as mentioned above, administrative penalties are 'efficient but are often adjudicated in ways that do not fully comply with

211 As opposed to market manipulation regulations, in which Article 176 and Article 178-2(2) set out near-identical rules aside from the existence of mental elements, insider trading regulations, as outlined in Article 174 and Article 178-2(1), differ significantly. The latter, exemplified by Article 178-2(1), extends its regulatory ambit beyond that of the former. For instance, it encompasses the regulation of remote tippees, a provision not applicable under Article 174. A detailed discussion on insider trading regulations is beyond the scope of this inquiry, but it can be argued that the complementary aspect of Article 178-2(1) is likely to be supplanted by a general anti-fraud provision, namely Article 178. See Lee (n 185) 119.

212 Supreme Court Decision 99Do2282 Decided 26 June 2021.

213 John C Coffee Jr, 'Paradigms Lost: The Blurring of the Criminal and Civil Law Models – And What Can Be Done About It' (1992) 101(8) Yale L J 1875, 1876.

procedural fairness'.[214] In particular, the challenges regarding fairness become more pronounced when the institutional design of the regulatory body is structured around an integrated model, 'centralising investigation, prosecution, and decision-making within a single entity'.[215] Such an organisational structure may compromise regulatory independence and impartiality, potentially leading to 'prosecutorial bias', where the adjudicator is more likely to favour conviction.[216] In this regard, the institutional arrangements and governance capacities for enforcement authorities in Korea seems to 'measure up, to some degree, the standard for ensuring fairness in administrative proceedings'.[217] The appointment process of commissioners of the FSC and guarantees of their tenure are considered adequate for ensuring the independence and neutrality of the public enforcer. However, the fact that all stages of the 'investigation, sanction proposal, and final decision-making' are processed in a single authority (the FSC and the Securities and Futures Commission therein), coupled with the hierarchical oversight of the supervisory agency (the Financial Supervisory Service) by the government authority, implies that the conclusions reached by the enforcer may lack objectivity and impartiality.[218] In order to resolve this issue, in fact, a revamp of financial supervisory architecture is necessary, which is a topic that falls outside the scope of this article. However, it may be argued that as a viable solution, 'the competent authority (in this case, the FSC) could effectively operate akin to a first-tier tribunal'.[219] This involves using the US SEC as a benchmark model, where an administrative law judge 'presides within the market authority to over trials as a finder of facts and adjudicate claims or disputes' related to regulatory matters, acting as a quasi-trial court judge.[220]

On a related note, some may argue that the latest ruling by the US Supreme Court will likely make this proposal much less tenable and unconvincing. On 27 June 2024, in a 6–3 decision, the highest court held in *SEC* v *Jarkesy* that the SEC's routine practice of 'imposing fines in its administrative proceedings, used to penalise securities fraud, violates the Seventh Amendment *right of trial*

214 Perrone (n 210) 386.
215 Ibid 387.
216 Ibid.
217 Kang (n 201) 535.
218 Ibid.
219 Ibid.
220 Ibid. For the record, the decision issued by the competition authority in Korea, the Fair Trade Commission (FTC), has the full force and effect of a trial court's verdict. In essence, the FTC operates as a quasi-judicial body.

by jury in all suits at common law'.[221] According to the Court's decision, the US government agency is not allowed to bring enforcement actions 'before intra-agency administrative law judges to seek civil penalties against individuals accused of violating the anti-fraud provisions of the federal securities laws'; defendants have the right to 'a trial by a jury of their peers before a neutral adjudicator' in federal court, not in a regulatory authority.[222] The judicial reasoning was based on the strict interpretation of the constitutional term 'public rights', which permits an exception to the application of the Seventh Amendment.[223] The majority of justices held that public rights exception applies 'only to the collection of revenue, customs enforcement, immigration, and grant of public benefits', illustrating some earlier cases upholding the doctrine, and the SEC's enforcement of the antifraud regulations fell outside this exception.[224] Moreover, they emphasised that civil monetary penalties the SEC imposes are 'designed to punish and deter, not to compensate' for losses incurred by victims, which represents 'a type of remedy at common law that could only be enforced in courts of law'.[225]A comprehensive discussion of the constitutional law theories and arguments is beyond the scope of this inquiry. However, it is likely that some plausible rebuttal exists. As Justice Sonia Sotomayor (joined by Justice Elena Kagan and Ketanji Brown Jackson) highlighted in her opinion for the dissent, the Court's narrow conception of the public rights exception seems to be erroneous because 'cases where the government itself is claimant (or a party) cannot be considered private disputes'.[226] Notably, as the majority argued, if the SEC's imposition of civil penalties is intended for punishment and deterrence of socially unacceptable practices, this indicates that the agency's claims against wrongdoers relate to the protection of public rights. Furthermore, it

221 Ronald Mann, 'Justices limit major SEC tool to penalise fraud' SCOTUSblog – *Opinion Analysis* (28 June 2024) https://www.scotusblog.com/case-files/cases/securities-and-exchange-commission-v-jarkesy/. For the full exposition of this ruling and details of the case, see 22–859 *SEC* v *Jarkesy* (2024) https://www.supremecourt.gov/opinions/23pdf/22-859new_kjfm.pdf.

222 Thomas P. DeFranco and others, 'SEC v. Jarkesy: Supreme Court Delivers Significant Blow to SEC Intra-Agency Enforcement' *Insights* (8 July 2024) https://www.dwt.com/blogs/financial-services-law-advisor/2024/07/takeaways-from-scotus-ruling-in-sec-v-jarkesy.

223 The public rights exception refers to the Court's recognition of the legislators' authority to 'assign the matter for decision to an agency without a jury, consistent with the Seventh Amendment'. Therefore, in matters concerning public rights, under Congress's delegated authority to enforce the law, the government agency can pursue claims for civil penalties through internal proceedings overseen by administrative law judges. See Mann (n 221).

224 Ibid.

225 DeFranco and others (n 222).

226 Mann (n 221).

can be argued that this ruling has disregarded the principle of *stare decisis* or respect for precedent, particularly the Court's decision in *Atlas Roofing Co.* v *Occupational Safety and Health Review Commission* that 'authorised a federal agency to adjudicate a statutory right that inheres in the government in its sovereign capacity'.[227] In a practical sense, the sharp decline in the SEC's use of administrative proceedings before administrative law judges could limit the agency's ability to combat market abuse considerably.[228] Given the greater expertise and experience that a regulatory authority possesses compared to courts, which I emphasise again, the harm would likely outweigh the benefits from such a drastic shift in enforcement policy.

Meanwhile, there might be a concern that the new approach to punishing an offender through both criminal and administrative sanctions on the basis of the same offence would likely violate the *ne bis in idem* (also known as the principle against double jeopardy) rule. Perhaps, more pertinent to this discussion would be a landmark EU case law development – the 2014 decision of the European Court of Human Rights (ECtHR) in the case *Grande Stevens et al* v *Italy*.[229] In *Grande Stevens*, the ECtHR ruled that 'offences punished by the two applicable laws and regulations by reason of a breach of rules based on the same fact constitute a violation of the *ne bis in idem* principle, no matter than sanctions are formally labelled as criminal or administrative' under the market abuse legislation.[230] In the court' opinion, the crux of the double jeopardy rule is to bar an identical prosecution for the same offence, and a formal classification of sanctions (i.e., naming as criminal or administrative punishments) is of

---

227 Ibid. The 1977 holding validated civil penalties that the government agency determined through internal proceedings. For details, see *Atlas Roofing Co. v. Occupational Safety Commission*, 430 U.S. 442, 97 S. Ct. 1261 (1977).

228 In fact, this concern extends beyond the SEC to numerous other federal agencies that use similar enforcement tools, raising the possibility that their administrative enforcement actions could also be 'susceptible to the argument that they have common law analogues and seek the imposition of remedies that are punitive in nature, requiring a jury'. DeFranco and others (n 222).

229 For full details of the facts of the case and the court's decision, see case of *Grande Stevens* v *Italy* (Application no 18640/10) ECtHR 4 March 2014; 7 July 2014 (Final).

230 Kang (n 201) 536. Relatedly, the preamble 23 of the Directive (EU) 2014/57 (on criminal sanctions of market abuse) states that 'the imposition of criminal sanctions for offences in accordance with this Directive and of administrative sanctions in accordance with the Regulation (EU) 596/2014 does not lead to a breach of the principle of *ne bis in idem*'. However, this ruling has given impetus for a radical rethink of the sanctions regime in the EU Member States for punishing market abuse. In actuality, after the decision in *Grande Stevens*, several similar outcomes were achieved. See Anita Clifford, 'Double Jeopardy and Concurrent Proceedings for Financial Wrongdoing' *Lexology Article* (11 September 2017) https://www.lexology.com/library/detail.aspx?g=3d69e4fe-c92c-4fb1-88b6-1ea4057a6405.

little consequence; rather, 'punitive nature of the offence and the severity of the punishment is substantively important for whether to classify sanctions as criminal or not'.[231]

Based on this European court's ruling, the recent amendment to the Korean securities law 'can be subject to criticism for having compromised the *ne bis in idem* principle'.[232] Formally naming the FSC's penalty surcharges as 'administrative' sanctions notwithstanding, from the viewpoints of the ECtHR, they have good reason to be classified as 'criminal' penalties, given that 'multiple of ill-gotten profits (avoided losses) shall be imposed as a penalty with a ceiling that may reach' KRW 4 billion.[233] Additionally, the new enforcement regime requires the market authority to take into account criminal sanctions already imposed by the judicial authorities, when charging its administrative penalties; per 429-2(2) of the FSCMA, once a criminal fine is imposed in a market abuse offence, administrative penalties may be waived, or a portion or the entirety of the fine, including any relevant confiscation or collections, can be deducted from such penalties. Of course, this measure is deliberately intended to circumvent the potential issue of *ne bis in idem* and the proportionality in punishment, but this is in marked contrast to the approach taken by the ECtHR, which held that 'the previously imposed sanctions when sentencing in subsequent proceedings is deemed to be irrelevant'.[234]

Nonetheless, it is important to acknowledge that a concurrent imposition of criminal and administrative sanctions does not contravene the principle of *ne bis in idem*. According to the Constitutional Court of Korea (헌법재판소), one of the highest courts along with the Supreme Court, the duplication of criminal sanctions and administrative penalties are possible under the Korean legal system, and it does not clearly conflict with the double jeopardy rule.[235] Likewise, the Korean Supreme Court has made it clear that administrative penalties in essence differ from criminal punishments as they aim at the disgorgement of illicit profits as well as serve to deter law violations. Thus, even if the law allows for parallel proceedings and the imposition of both criminal

231 Kang (n 201) 536.

232 Ibid.

233 Ibid.

234 Ibid. For reference, the Korean legislators had sought to minimise potential controversies regarding double jeopardy in the imposition of sanctions, indeed. See Political Affairs Committee, *Review Report on Partially Amended Financial Investment Services and Capital Markets Act* (Bill No 2103921, June 2023).

235 Constitutional Court Decision 2001Hun-Ka25 Decided 24 July 2003.

and administrative penalties, such actions may not be deemed a violation of the *ne bis in idem* principle.[236]

4.3 *A Need to Fill the Regulatory Voids in Algorithmic and High-Frequency Trading*

4.3.1 Background Arguments

The last issue of concern relates to technological advancements in trading tactics, most notably algorithmic and high-frequency trading, which have radically transformed the landscape and dynamics of trading over recent decades. Algorithmic trading (AT) refers to 'trading in financial instruments where a computer algorithm (the execution algorithm) automatically determines order specifications, such as when to initiate the order, the price or quantity of the order and how to manage the order after it is submitted, with limited or no human intervention'.[237] High-frequency trading (HFT) is an extension of algorithmic trading, 'where more complexity and speed are usually involved'.[238] In this new financial reality, as evidenced by the 2010 flash crash, significant sums of capital can vanish within moments, a small group of traders can impede or disturb the entire trading operations, and rogue actors may rig trillion-dollar markets opportunistically 'with a simple click or a few lines of code'.[239] As such, regulators are now confronted with an unprecedented mode of market manipulation. Indeed, as the highly sophisticated AT and HFT traders have grown their presence and gained further influence in the markets, enforcement

236 Supreme Court Decision 2001Du6197 Decided 9 April 2004. The highest courts' analysis as such is consistent with that of the US judicial precedents, such as *Hudson* v *United States*, 522 US 93 (1997). For a similar decision, see also *SEC* v *Gordon*, 822 F. Supp. 2d 1144 (N.D. Okla. 2011).

237 European Central Bank (ECB), 'Algorithmic trading : trends and existing regulation' *Newsletter articles* (13 February 2019) https://www.bankingsupervision.europa.eu/press/publications/newsletter/2019/html/ssm.nl190213_5.en.html.

238 Ibid. Relatedly, the US regulatory body (in this case, the CFTC) provide more concrete terms, explaining that the attributes of HFT include: (i) algorithms for decision making, order initiation, generation, routing, or execution, for each individual transaction without human direction; (ii) low-latency technology that is designed to minimise response times, including proximity and co-location services; (iii) high speed connections to markets for order entry; and (iv) recurring high message rates (orders, quotes or cancellations) determined using one or more objective forms of measurement. See CFTC, 'A Proposed Rule: Concept Release on Risk Controls and System Safeguards for Automated Trading Environments' 78 Fed Reg 56542 (12 September 2013).

239 Tom C. Lin, 'New Market Manipulation' (2017) 66(6) Emory L J 1253, 1255.

authorities are increasingly grappling with these new types of regulatory challenges.[240]

In particular, the ultra-high speed (typically measured in milliseconds) processing and massive volume of trades powered by algorithmic and high-frequency trading can potentially give rise to the systemic risk of 'too fast to save': that is, it may raise the likelihood that 'inadvertent error, malicious acts and technological disruptions would harm the financial institutions and financial system' before timely interventions are implemented.[241] Moreover, due to these incredibly high velocities, it poses a significant challenge for regulators in detecting ongoing market manipulation schemes.[242] Further, the heavy reliance of AT and HFT on autonomous computerised systems, with minimal or no human intervention, makes it tough for enforcement authorities to attribute culpability or liability to the person involved in suspected schemes. This is because the mental element, such as manipulative intent, has long been an essential ingredient of market manipulation offences under traditional legal interpretations.[243] In addition, unfair or unjust trading issue may arise, due to the opportunities presented by HFT, enabling 'a limited number of traders to beat the market by exploiting the time advantage accrued through the use of algorithms, faster networks, and co-location'.[244] In other words, only a specific cohort of 'professional, highly specialised HFT traders' can consistently 'outmanoeuvre traditional investors' in the unlevel playing field.[245]

Of course, algorithmic and high-frequency trading has its own merits as well as drawbacks referred to above, just like every coin has two sides. Among other things, it has the effect of reducing bid-ask spreads, thus lowering the cost of liquidity. Also, by minimising slippage in trading, investors are able to 'execute trades almost instantaneously, without fear that prices or other information

240 High-frequency trading is purported to 'have accounted for 35% to 40% of all European equity trading and 60% of all US equity trading'. See Ibid 1296–1297.

241 Ibid 1273.

242 Ibid 1296.

243 Ibid 1301. This issue becomes more pronounced when it concerns establishing criminal liability. For the relevant discussion, see Orlando Cosme Jr., 'Regulating High-Frequency Trading: The Case for Individual Criminal Liability' (2019) 109(2) J Crim. L & Criminology 365.

244 Megan Woodward, 'The Need for Speed: Regulatory Approaches to High Frequency Trading in the United States and the European Union' (2021) 50 Vanderbilt Law Rev 1359, 1376–1377.

245 Ibid. According to a recent study that 'analysed CFTC audit-level trading data' in a certain futures market, it was found that HFT orders 'generate valuable private information'.

will grow stale before their orders go through.'[246] Undoubtedly, HFT's 'ability to readjust orders' at full tilt in response to evolving market conditions may be beneficial to both the investing public and the whole market system in terms of enhancing price discovery function.[247] Hence, market authorities in major jurisdictions, including the US and the EU, seek to balance between the competing benefits and risks associated with AT and HFT by implementing adequate rules and regulations.

4.3.2 The US Approach to HFT Regulation

The US regulation of algorithmic and high-frequency trading is particularly featured by its heightened focus on preserving market stability and integrity.[248] Key bedrock rules include the 'Market Access Rule' (Rule 15c3-5) implemented in 2010 and the 'Regulation Systems Compliance and Integrity' (Reg SCI) that was introduced in 2014. Rule 15c3-5 under the Exchange Act requires 'firms with market access or that provide market access to their customers to appropriately control the risks associated with market access' especially for the purpose of maintaining 'the integrity of trading on the securities markets and the stability of the financial system'.[249] Specifically, pursuant to this rule, such firms are obliged to 'establish, document, and maintain a system of risk management controls and supervisory procedures that are reasonably designed to (i) systematically limit the financial exposure of the broker or dealer that could arise as a result of market access, and (ii) ensure compliance with all regulatory requirements that are applicable in connection with market access'.[250] Relatedly, this set of rules includes measures such as 'preventing the entry of orders that exceed appropriate pre-set credit or capital thresholds, or that appear to be erroneous', and 'restricting market access technology and systems to authorised persons'.[251]

246 Charles R Korsmo, 'High-frequency Trading: A Regulatory Strategy' (2014) 48(2) U Rich L Rev, 523, 549.

247 Ibid 550.

248 Gaia Balp and Giovanni Strampelli, 'Preserving Capital Markets Efficiency in the High-Frequency Trading Era' (2018) 2018(2) U Ill J L Tech & Pol'y 349, 365.

249 Financial Industry Regulatory Authority (FINRA), '2022 Report on FINRA's Examination and Risk Monitoring Program' (9 February 2022) https://www.finra.org/rules-guidance/guidance/reports/2022-finras-examination-and-risk-monitoring-program/market-access-rule.

250 SEC, 'Final Rule: Risk Management Controls for Brokers or Dealers with Market Access' Release No. 34-63241; File No. S7-03-10 (3 November 2010) https://www.sec.gov/files/rules/final/2010/34-63241.pdf.

251 Ibid.

Regulation SCI was adopted with a view to reinforcing 'the technology infrastructure of US securities markets'.[252] Primarily directed at entities involved in 'trading, market data processing, market regulation, market surveillance, clearing and settlement, and order routing', this regulation requires these entities to mitigate and manage operational risks associated with their systems, aiming at preventing 'the occurrence of systems issues, and improving resilience when systemic problems do occur'.[253] To this end, it mandates their 'participation in testing business continuity and disaster recovery plans', which includes obligating those firms to 'take corrective action and disseminate information' regarding systems disruptions and problems.[254]

In addition to these, rules and regulations have been consistently reinforced to enhance transparency and contain the risks of AT and HFT. By virtue of the 2015 amendment to Rule 15b9-1, the previous exempt HFT firms were required to 'register with Financial Industry Regulatory Authority (FINRA), and thus face FINRA's regulatory oversight'.[255] Through the 2010 implementation of the 'stub quotes ban', the SEC has 'reduced the risk of trades being executed at irrational prices'.[256] The limit up-limit down (LULD) mechanism was introduced in 2012 with the aim of 'stopping excess volatility in a single stock'.[257] While akin to the existing circuit-breakers mechanism in temporarily restricting trades beyond preset price bands, the LULD rule diverges in its focus, as it specifically addresses the price volatilities of individual stocks, in contrast to the broader scope of the circuit-breakers trading curb, which encompasses market-wide price movements.[258] While initially adopted, on a pilot basis, by the SEC, the measure was approved as a permanent rule in 2019.

Meanwhile, manipulative trades using AT and HFT in securities markets is regulated by the existing market abuse rules (i.e., Section 10(b) of the Exchange

252 Woodward (n 244) 1378.

253 Ibid.

254 Ibid.

255 Ibid 1381.

256 SEC, Press Release: SEC Approves New Rules Prohibiting Market Maker Stub Quotes (8 November 2010) https://www.sec.gov/news/press/2010/2010-216.htm. The new regulation has mandated market makers to issue quotes that are 'within a certain percentage band of the national best bid and offer (NBBO)'.

257 Phil Mackintosh, 'All about LULDS' *NASDAQ News & Insights* (10 February 2022) https://www.nasdaq.com/articles/all-about-lulds.

258 The calculation of price bands relies on 'a reference price – the arithmetic mean price over the prior five-minute period', with the bands established 'at a specified percentage level above and below the reference price'. When the price touches the bands (thus, entering a 'limit state') and persists for more than 15 seconds, trading halts for five minutes. See Ibid.

Act and SEC Rule 10-5), and the same conduct in commodities derivatives markets is prohibited by the CEA. On a related note, there are 'a few of the more common and prominent methods' of manipulation scheme (which include 'pinging, spoofing (or layering), electronic front running'), and spoofing, *inter alia*, has attracted intense scrutiny from federal financial regulators due to concerns regarding its enforceability.[259] Spoofing refers to 'bidding or offering with the intention to cancel the bid or offer before execution'.[260] By intentionally placing '*non-bona fide* orders', such scheme has the potential to 'trick and induce other market participants to execute' trades with the expectation of capitalising on changes in the order book.[261] As such, not a few rulings by US courts have concluded that spoofing can contravene the anti-fraud provisions of federal securities laws.[262] Spoofing is also deemed to be a disruptive trading practice. By submitting or cancelling (multiple) bids or offers, it can 'overload the quote system of a registered entity, delay another person's execution trades, create an appearance of false market depth, and create artificial price movements'.[263] Thus, Section 4c(a)(5)(C) of the CEA explicitly outlaws spoofing.[264] Further, the *Coscia* decision in 2016 made it clear that HFT traders engaging in spoofing strategies could face criminal convictions.[265]

However, enforcing the 'spoofing prohibition against speed-driven HFT' can be an unwieldy task due to the necessity of demonstrating 'intent', which

259 Lin (n 239) 1288. Pinging involves the submission of 'a large number of small orders for a particular financial instrument, cancelled in fractions of a second' by computerised systems to gauge the reactions from other market participants, 'inducing them to disclose their trading intentions in response' to the signals (pings). Electronic front running is an order anticipation strategy, in which HFT traders 'gain an unfair glimpse into order flows at one trading venue' and are *en route* to other trading venues to leverage their speed advantages. Layering, a form of spoofing, refers to placing a sequence of spoof orders at various price levels increasingly moving away from the prevailing market price.

260 CFTC, 'Fact Sheet: Interpretive Guidance and Policy Statement on Disruptive practices' (28 May 2013) https://www.cftc.gov/sites/default/files/idc/groups/public/@newsroom/documents/file/dtp_factsheet.pdf.

261 Rahman Ravelli (n 79) 16–17.

262 See e.g., *SEC* v *Lek Sec. Corp.*, 276 F. Supp. 3d 49 (S.D.N.Y. 2017); *CP Stone Fort Holdings, LLC* v *Doe*, Case No. 16 C 4991 (N.D. Ill. 22 Mar 2017); see also SEC's Litigation Release No 25319 (26 January 2022), *United States* v *Milrud*, No 2:15-cv-00237 (DNJ filed January 13, 2015).

263 CFTC (n 260).

264 7 USC § 6c(a)(5)(C). The enactment of this statutory provision, which bans the 'spoofing' strategy by name for the first time, occurred via the 2012 amendment to the CEA under Section 747 of the Dodd-Frank Act.

265 *United States* v *Coscia*, 100 F. Supp. 3d 653 (N.D. Ill. 2015), *aff'd*, 177 F. Supp. 3d 1087 (N.D. Ill. 2016). Michael Coscia, known as 'the first defendant in the US to stand trial under Dodd-Frank anti-spoofing legislation', received a three-year prison sentence and two years of supervised release.

entails a mental state beyond recklessness, in order to establish the offence.[266] Given the fact that there are various legitimate order cancellation types, including 'fill or kill' (FOK) order and 'immediate or cancel' (IOC) order, in particular, identifying the unlawful element within generally accepted market practices can be even more challenging.[267]

4.3.3 The EU Approach to HFT Regulation

It is well accepted that the EU regulations of algorithmic and high-frequence trading are 'comprehensive and, at least to some extent, very detailed'.[268] Indeed, an extensive set of rules and requirements relating to AT and HFT is outlined in the revised Markets in Financial Instruments Directive (MiFID II) and the Regulation on Market Abuse (MAR).[269] Out of these rules, some bear a close resemblance to those implemented in the US; both sides of the Atlantic

266 CFTC, 'Anti-disruptive Practices Authority' 78 Fed Reg 31890, 31892, 31896 (28 May 2013).

267 A fill or kill (FOK) order is an order that 'must be executed immediately in its entirety; otherwise, the entire order will be cancelled', whereas an immediate or cancel (IOC) order is 'an order to buy or sell a stock that must be executed immediately and any portion that cannot be filled immediately will be cancelled (i.e., a partial execution of the order is allowed)'. See the website of the SEC's Office of Investor Education and Advocacy https://www.investor.gov/introduction-investing/investing-basics/glossary.

268 Marus Lerch, 'Algorithmic Trading and High-Frequency Trading' in Rüdiger Veil (ed), European Capital Markets Law (3rd edn, Hart 2022) 493. At a national level, stricter rules than at the Union level are implemented. For example, Germany has enacted its own High-Frequency Trading Act, which includes 'licensing' requirements, 'minimum capital' requirements and specific 'reporting and disclosure' requirements for HFT firms. Also, France has imposed a tax on orders that are 'modified or cancelled, provided they exceed 80% of all orders transmitted in a month', in case where HFT firms engage in order transmission, modification, or cancellation 'within a timeframe of 500 milliseconds'. See ibid 488. However, a detailed examination of the HFT regulations set forth by each Member State is beyond the scope of this inquiry. For a more comprehensive investigation of the regulatory landscape of HFT across the globe, see Holly A Bell and Harrison Searles, 'An Analysis of Global HFT Regulation – Motivations, Market Failures, and Alternative Outcomes' (1 April 2014) *Mercatus Center Working Paper* No 14-11 http://dx.doi.org/10.2139/ssrn.2689321.

269 MiFID II (2014/65/EU), which denotes the amendments to Markets in Financial Instruments Directive (2004/39/EC), originally introduced in 2007 under the name MiFID I, came into effect on 3 January 2018. The EU legislation was designed to 'develop a more harmonised set of financial regulation and ensure a high level of investor protection across the Union'. See Recital of the MiFID II https://www.esma.europa.eu/publications-and-data/interactive-single-rulebook/mifid-ii. Market Abuse Regulation (Regulation (EU) 596/2014), which repealed and replaced the previous Market Abuse Directive (Directive 2003/6/EC) from 3 July 2016, as aforementioned, aims to promote market integrity and investor protection by prohibiting abusive trading practices such as insider dealing and market manipulation.

share common regulatory terms and standards in defining parameters related to AT and HFT.[270] For example, as with the US rules, MiFID II characterises HFT as an algorithmic trading technique having the following attributes:

(i) infrastructure intended to minimise network and other types of latencies through at least one of the facilities for algorithmic order entry such as co-location, proximity hosting, or high-speed direct electronic access;

(ii) system determines order initiation, generation, routing or execution without human intervention; and

(iii) high message intraday rates which constitute orders, quotes or cancellations.[271]

Moreover, mirroring the 'emphasis on potential systemic risks' seen in US regulations, the EU legislation seeks to subject AT and HFT to special supervision.[272] In actuality, the EU regime imposes 'far-reaching responsibilities on trading venues' in relation to their internal systems and controls.[273] More specifically, aside from the general requirements ensuring the soundness and competence of their trading systems for exchange markets, trading venues accommodating AT and HFT traders assume some additional responsibilities.[274] On a related note, a trading venue is required to implement 'effective systems, procedures and arrangements to reject orders that exceed pre-determined volume and price thresholds or are clearly erroneous'.[275] Additionally, it should be able to 'temporarily halt or constrain trading' in the event of an abrupt price swings in

270 Woodward (n 244) 1389.

271 Art 4(1)(40) Directive 2014/65/EU. With respect to the requirement at (iii) of 'high message intraday rates', the Commission Delegated Regulation supplementing MiFID II clarified that the stipulation of the MiFID II definition 'consists of (i) at least two messages per second with respect to any single financial instrument traded on a trading venue; and (ii) at least four messages per second with respect to all financial instruments traded on a trading venue' (Art 19(1) Regulation (EU) 2017/565).

272 Lerch (n 268) 489.

273 Danny Busch, 'MiFID II: regulating high frequency trading, other forms of algorithmic trading and direct electronic market access' (2016) 10(2) Law Financ Mark Rev 72, 79.

274 Article 48(1) of MiFID II stipulates that a regulated market is basically required to 'have in place effective systems, procedures and arrangements to ensure its trading systems are (i) resilient, (ii) have sufficient capacity to deal with peak order and message volumes, (iii) are able to ensure orderly trading under conditions of severe market stress, (iv) are fully tested to ensure such conditions are met and (v) are subject to effective business continuity arrangements to ensure continuity of its services if there is any failure of its trading systems'. Per Article 18(5) of MiFID II, these requirements extend to multilateral trading facilities (MTFs) and organised trading facilities (OTFs).

275 Art 48(4) Directive 2014/65/EU.

a financial instrument, and in exceptional circumstances, to be able to 'cancel, vary or correct any transaction'.[276]

In addressing concerns regarding the orderly and fair-trading conditions, the EU law also 'sets out in detail organisational requirements that must be fulfilled by trading venues'.[277] Pursuant to the relevant provisions, a trading venue is required to operate its system in a manner that permits 'direct electronic access' (DEA) exclusively to members and other entities who have met obligations and criteria stipulated in the law and have 'retained responsibility for orders and trades executed using that service'.[278] Furthermore, a trading venue is mandated to ensure that co-location services are offered 'on non-discriminatory, fair and transparent basis'.[279] The EU legislation also requires a trading venue to design its fee structures with transparency, fairness, and non-discrimination, particularly ensuring they do not 'incentivise the placement, modification, or cancellation of orders, or the execution of transactions in a way which contributes to disorderly trading conditions or market abuse'.[280] Relatedly, a trading venue may 'adjust its fees for cancelled orders' based on the duration for which the orders are held, and 'calibrate the fees to each financial instrument to which they apply'.[281] In other words, a trading venue is allowed to impose a higher fee under the following circumstances: (i) 'for placing an order that is subsequently cancelled than an order which is executed', (ii) 'on participants placing a high ratio of cancelled orders to executed orders' and (iii) 'on those operating a high-frequency algorithmic trading technique in order to reflect the additional burden on system capacity'.[282]

MiFID II imposes a set of detailed rules and requirements on HFT firms as well. The internal systems and controls of such firms must meet qualifications analogous to those imposed on trading venues referred to above; that is, HFT firms are obligated to ensure that their trading systems are robust enough to be 'resilient', 'have sufficient capacity', and 'prevent the systems otherwise functioning in a way that may create or contribute to a disorderly market'.[283] In addition to these, investment firms employing HFT strategies have certain

276 Art 48(5) Directive 2014/65/EU.

277 Busch (n 273) 78.

278 A regulated market may 'suspend or terminate the provision of direct electronic access by a member or participant to a client in the case of non-compliance with' the requirements (Art 48(7) Directive 2014/65/EU).

279 Art 48(8) and Art 18(5) Directive 2014/65/EU.

280 Art 48(9) and Art 18(5) Directive 2014/65/EU.

281 Ibid.

282 Ibid.

283 Art 17(1) Directive 2014/65/EU.

duties to fulfil in addressing concerns related to trading opacity, which includes, *inter alia*, maintaining records and timely reporting the relevant information to market authorities. Those obligations are essential not only for resolving transparency concerns and the resulting lack of trust in market institutions but also for improving the regulatory efficacy. Notably, for this purpose, the EU law confers upon the competent authorities of Member States extensive powers to request information from investment firms involved in HFT activities. Per Article 17(2) of MiFID II, financial regulators of home Member State of the HFT firm 'may require the investment firm to provide, on a regular or ad-hoc basis, a description of the nature of its algorithmic trading strategies, details of the trading parameters or limits to which the system is subject, the key compliance and risk controls that it has in place'. Further, the market authority retains the authority to, at any time, request additional information 'from an investment firm about its algorithmic trading and the systems used for that trading'.[284] Besides, given the prevalence of cross-exchange trades in HFT, the information obtained by the NCA of home Member State as such is mandated to be conveyed promptly upon 'request by the competent authority of the trading venue without undue delay'.[285]

Meanwhile, as discussed in the previous section (see Section 3.2.1), the EU law has established new rules specifically targeting algorithmic and high frequency trading in its Market Abuse Regulation (MAR) provision. Under Article 12(2)(c) of MAR, engaging in activities of placing, cancelling, or modifying orders through 'electronic means, such as algorithmic and high-frequency trading strategies', which can result in manipulative effects causing harm to market integrity, constitutes illegal market manipulation. Interestingly, this European approach contrasts with that of US law, which seeks to address new technology-induced market abuse behaviours through existing securities laws and regulations, without the addition of tailored regulatory tools. Certainly, there are likely numerous reasons for such a distinction. However, it is conceivable that this discrepancy is partly attributed to the differences between the legal systems: that is, the distinction between civil law, characterised by 'comprehensive and continuously updated legal codes that specify all matters capable of being brought before a court', and the common law tradition, which relies heavily on 'precedent rather than a comprehensive compilation of legal rules and statutes'.[286]

284 Art 17(2) Directive 2014/65/EU.

285 Ibid.

286 A more detailed explanation of these two legal systems is available on the Berkeley Law website https://www.law.berkeley.edu/wp-content/uploads/2017/11/CommonLawCivilLawTraditions.pdf.

4.3.4 The Korean Approach to HFT Regulation: Current Status and Way Forward

The preceding discussion reveals the fact that major jurisdictions such as the US and the EU have enacted statutes and regulations specifically targeting algorithmic and high-frequency trading activities. However, the Korean law – in this case, the Capital Markets Act (자본시장과 금융투자업에 관한 법률) – is silent on that issue; instead, the regulatory system tackles the issues related to AT and HFT mainly through Korea Exchange (KRX) guidelines and its internal business regulations.[287] KRX established its 'guidelines on risk management of algorithm trading' in November 2014 for the first time to regulate the member firms' trading practices, which largely mirrored HFT rules regarding automated systems and controls seen in the US and the EU. Nonetheless, it is, if anything, a mere code of conduct solely for KRX's members, not a statutory regulation. Thus, there is much criticism that its usefulness is inherently limited.[288]

More recently, on 7 December 2022, KRX amended its securities and derivatives market business regulations to refine its AT, in particular, high-speed AT (or HFT) rules. According to the new KRX's AT-HFT regulations, any investors who engage in 'high-speed algorithmic trading in the markets must register in advance with the KRX through member firms' for KRX to 'assign identification codes to registered such HFT traders and monitor their trades' (Per Section 104–3 of KOSPI market business regulation; 유가증권시장 업무규정).[289] Also, the revised rules require member firms to 'conduct inspection of the relevant customer's electronic systems including ordering system and risk management' and, upon KRX's request, to 'submit the relevant information for the purpose of checking whether the members' obligation is satisfied and managing the market' (Per Section 104–4 of KOSPI market business regulation).

However, it can be argued that the ongoing regulatory efforts are still not enough to cope with potential risks of AT and HFT, because such an entire reliance on the rules of self-regulatory organisation may cause many problems

287 KRX is currently the sole bourse operator and a self-regulatory organisation in Korea.

288 GiJin Yang, 'Limitations and Improvement Plans of Regulation of Market Manipulative Behaviours using High Frequency Algorithm under the Current Korean Law' (2023) 13(2) J Fin Consum 107, 116.

289 Korea Exchange (KRX), Press Release: Notice of Revision of Securities and Derivatives Market Business Regulations to Manage High-Speed Algorithmic Traders (25 October 2022). Under Section 104–3(5) of the KRX regulation, when a member's customer fails to meet the certain conditions (e.g., having 'suitable computers system' and 'sufficient knowledge and experience') required for conducting high-speed algorithmic trading, the member should take appropriate measures, such as 'refusing to receive orders for high-speed trading submitted by the customer or closing entire accounts opened for the relevant customers'. For more details, see the KRX website https://sribond.krx.co.kr/en/05/05040000/SRI05040000.jsp.

in terms of law enforcement. Among other things, regulatory intervention in HFT matters is only possible *via* KRX members; there is no effective means for market authorities to directly discipline and sanction non-members.[290] More fundamentally, KRX business regulations are designed to 'stipulate the (general) matters necessary for the trading of securities' in exchange markets, and accordingly they are not suitable for regulating market abuse behaviours such as manipulative trading.[291] Furthermore, delegating regulatory responsibilities to member firms that are in a fiduciary relationship with HFT traders would likely risk creating conflicts of interest.[292] Accordingly, it is recommended that the Capital Markets Act be revised to empower market authorities to impose the relevant regulatory obligations directly on high-speed algorithmic traders and administer appropriate sanctions when deemed necessary.

There might be a question regarding whether Article 178 or Article 178-2 of the FSCMA could potentially be applicable to cases involving market abuse offences associated with algorithmic and high-frequency trading. In fact, Article 178(1) is the general anti-fraud provision of the Korean securities law, and hence it may, in principle, cover any financial misconduct utilising new financial technologies. However, as previously discussed in Section 3.3.1, the Korean courts are cautious about invoking the provision, in practice, for its risk of vagueness and overbreadth, considering other substantive rules directed at market abuse behaviours (i.e., Article 176 for market manipulation) first. In this context, Article 178-2(2) seems more likely applicable to such cases. The language used in the statutory provision apparently describes the illegal HFT practices, such as stub quotes and spoofing.[293] Nonetheless, the problem is that, as with Article 178, it does not expressly and explicitly define AT or HFT activities, nor delineates the elements constituting market manipulation driven by them. Additionally, in the absence of the relevant court cases and judicial interpretations thereof, enforcement authorities face difficulties in applying the law to these new types of financial wrongdoing.

The most recent case of Citadel Securities in Korea sheds light on how daunting a task sanctioning suspicious high-frequency algorithmic trading activities would be. On 26 January 2023, the Securities and Futures Commission (SFC), 'a sub-commission of the FSC responsible for the oversight of the securities and

290 Yang (n 288) 135.

291 See Section 1 of KOSPI market business regulation.

292 Yang (n 288) 118.

293 The first subparagraph of Article 178-2(2) provides for a prohibition against 'submitting a large volume of asking prices at which deals are unlikely to be concluded, or by repeatedly correcting or cancelling asking prices after submitting them'.

derivatives market', has imposed a penalty surcharge of KRW 11.9 billion (or USD 9.7 million) on Citadel Securities for having breached the regulation on market disturbances (Article 178-2(2)) pursuant to Article 429-2 of the FSCMA.[294] According to the market authority, the US-based investment firm engaged in disruptive activities to the marketplace while trading a total of 264 stock items in 6,796 trading periods between October 2017 and May 2018.[295] More specifically, the securities firm used the high-speed algorithmic tactics to (i) place immediate-or-cancel (IOC) market orders that are 'of sufficient quantity to sweep the entire quantity on the book', and (ii) generate a new best bid price with any remaining quantity from the aggressive submission of limit orders, and then cancel such transactions.[296] In the regulatory authority's perspective, such trading patterns amount to breach of the statutory regulation, since they were 'likely to artificially change market prices and trading volumes' and 'potentially mislead other investors to trade' stock items in question, thereby having undermined market integrity.[297]

This is the first instance the Korean government authorised the imposition of administrative sanction on a financial institution for market disorder caused by high-frequency algorithmic trading.[298] However, the process of reaching a sanctioning decision has not proceeded smoothly; since the investigation initially commenced in April 2019, there has been much discussion and deliberation, including several times of hearings and expert evidence.[299] In particular, there was intense controversy over the applicability of the current Capital Markets Act to AT and HFT activities. This is primarily because market abuse offences generally require a mental element but 'the use of high-speed and automated computer programmes generate, rout and execute orders and make trade decisions' with little or no human intervention.[300] For this reason, the market authority has determined to invoke Article 178-2(2), which does not require a demonstration of specific intent or purpose to establish a violation of

294 FSC, Press Release: SFC Imposes Penalty Surcharge on Overseas-based Financial Investment Entity for Market Disturbance (26 January 2023).

295 Ibid.

296 Ibid. According to the SFC inspection, at around 10:00 AM on a certain date of May 2018, the investment firm 'submitted a total of 34 IOC buy orders for a certain stock item – including 19 market orders to exhaust all quantities of best ask prices and 15 limit bid orders intended to fill gaps between the then best ask and bid price – which consequently pushed up the market price' of a target issue around 3.5% in a matter of one minute.

297 Ibid.

298 Ibid.

299 Ibid.

300 Yang (n 288) 122.

the law, in contrast to Articles 176 and 178, which necessitate proving a state of mind to punish the offender. Nonetheless, Citadel Securities disputed the allegations and the SFC's sanction decision, contending that the trading strategies concerned are 'the same as those that have been used in many markets around the world for years', and that the investment firm 'strongly believes its trading complied with both Korean laws and global norms'.[301] Eventually, the firm has sought to appeal the decision, and the litigation is now brought before the Seoul Administrative Court.

It becomes clear then that a complete reliance on self-regulation no longer holds, and the Korean legal system must introduce statutory regulations specifically addressing algorithmic and high-frequency trading. To this end, among other things, it is crucial for the Capital Markets Act (or FSCMA) to define the term AT and HFT clearly and to delineate parameters that outline the elements constituting market abuse offences, particularly, market manipulation. For this purpose, the EU law, MiFID II and MAR outlined above would be a good reference. Simply put, the relevant regulatory obligations or requirements should be placed on investment firms using high-frequency algorithmic trading technique in accordance with the revised statute regulation. If such an amendment to the FSCMA is enacted, market authorities would be better equipped to monitor the markets and prevent misconducts of HFT traders more effectively by direct imposition of the sanctions on offenders.[302]

In light of the growing discontent of the investing public regarding issues of unfairness and injustice, nevertheless, it can be asserted that such a reform is not enough, necessitating further regulations.[303] For example, some commentators argue that implementing 'minimum resting times', which dictate the duration for which a limit order must remain in force (i.e., prohibits its cancellation, within, *circa* 500 milliseconds of submission), is required to 'curb the excessive use of cancelled orders by HFT firms'.[304] To be sure, it

301 Jihoon Lee, 'S. Korea fines Citadel Securities for stock algorithm trading breaches' *Reuters* (27 January 2023) https://www.reuters.com/business/finance/skorea-fines-citadel-securities-stock-algorithm-trading-breaches-2023-01-27/.

302 Yang (n 288) 120.

303 The FSC acknowledges the widespread adoption of high-frequency algorithmic trading techniques in markets and the growing concerns about its associated risks and the potential for unfair trading practices. see FSC (n 294).

304 Mary Jo White, a former chair of the US SEC, expressed her qualified endorsement of this rule at the Sandler O'Neill & Partners, L.P. Global Exchange and Brokerage Conference: Enhancing Our Equity Market Structure, Speech (5 June 2014). See Michael Morelli, 'Implementing High Frequency Trading Regulation: A Critical Analysis of Current Reforms' (2017) 6(2) Mich Bus & Entrepreneurial L Rev 201, 203.

will disincentivise HFT traders to submit fictitious or fraudulent orders since such a delay 'makes the limit order more risky from an adverse selection standpoint'.[305] However, it should be noted that this restrictive measure also entails the risk of recklessly disregarding many legitimate trading activities of HFT firms to cancel stale orders and reconstruct order books, thus impairing market efficiency. Moreover, given the significant risks of adverse execution and the associated costs in terms of liquidity provision, spreads may widen, leading to a deterioration in overall market quality.[306] Further, if anything, HFT firms could only implement trading strategies 'at slower, but just as harmful intervals'.[307] Therefore, it seems undesirable to implement such a measure, and this would also be unfavourable to the overall interests of general investors. By the same token, when it comes to establishing the principle of 'non-discrimination' in securities markets, creating a level playing field among groups of investors should not be misconstrued as requiring 'all market participants to act at the same speed in practice'.[308] To the extent that any person willing to subscribe to 'latency-reducing services (such as co-location)' can enter into relevant arrangements with market venues, the market structure is, if nothing else, deemed 'fair from a procedural standpoint'.[309]

Meanwhile, HFT firms may well harbour concerns regarding the requirement to provide their source codes and details of information about HFT strategies upon request by market authorities. Despite that these are for the regulatory purposes, the automated systems and computerised programmes designed by a HFT firm 'form the core of its business model', and thus 'keeping the source codes secret' constitutes its competitive edge.[310] Besides, it is unclear whether regulators have sufficient knowledge or experience to disentangle algorithms. Nevertheless, such private interest might be subordinated to the public interest inevitably in certain circumstances, particularly when the financial markets appear to be vulnerable to flash crash dynamics or manipulative tactics. Furthermore, it is worth noting that regulators can 'achieve the correct level of knowledge and expertise only through far-reaching cooperation

305 Ibid.

306 Merritt B Fox and others, 'The New Stock Market: Sense and Nonsense' (2015) 65(2) Duke L J 191, 268–269.

307 It needs to be reminded that the EU authority rejected this form of speed bump measure following an extensive consultation process for the very reason. Morelli (n 304) 203–204.

308 Lerch (n 268) 492.

309 Ibid.

310 Busch (n 273) 76.

and the exchange of information' with the industry itself as well as with other government agencies.[311]

5 Concluding Remarks

One of the primary functions of financial markets is to gather all relevant information from market participants and discover a clearing price that reflects legitimate forces of supply and demand in the marketplace. Each investor sends her signal as to the value assessment of a financial instrument to the market, and the fair price is determined through the coordination of interplay between buyers and sellers. In such an equilibrium state, market efficiency is maximised; financial markets channel funds to instruments that will provide the highest rate of return for investors. However, there are prerequisites that must be in place so that financial markets can function properly: market integrity and investor trust. Market participants must be able to have confidence in efficiency and fairness of markets which they invest in, and also have trust in market institution (e.g., a certain degree of legal protection from securities fraud). Needless to say, investors will leave the market when they lose their faith in market system, or otherwise, even if they do not actually leave, deterioration in market quality will be inevitable. In this respect, banning market manipulation that could potentially undermine market integrity is both reasonable and justifiable insofar as they do not hinder ordinary (or generally accepted) trading activities.

However, as seen in this inquiry, regulating market manipulation proves to be a daunting task. Above all, distinguishing between legitimate speculation and illegal manipulation poses a substantial challenge in practice, as actual trades investors undertake often share the facially same characteristics. For this reason, demonstrating an inducement (of others to trade) is commonly deemed necessary to establish market manipulation offences, but the legal standard lacks precision and is prone to ambiguity in delineating its contours. Adding to the complexity is the reliance on circumstantial evidence in most market manipulation cases, where proofs are predominantly based on inference. Thus, it is argued here that a 'fraudulent' inducement, which is triggered by a manipulator's dissemination of misinformation that has the effect of sending misleading signals to the markets, plays a pivotal role in both defining market manipulation and establishing its regulatory perimeters.

311 Ibid.

Meanwhile, trading financial instruments are protean in nature. In continuously evolving and innovating market environments, new forms of trading tactics (including manipulative schemes) are consistently emerging and becoming more widely used. It is not surprising that the acceleration of the phenomenon wherein regulation and legislation lag behind market innovation is creating regulatory gaps within the financial industry. Notably, as argued before, the use of AT and HFT presents a significant challenge to enforcement authorities due to their reliance on automated computerised systems with minimal human intervention. This makes it tough for regulators to enforce market abuse regulations that traditionally necessitate a demonstrable mental state element. In this regard, the EU market manipulation rules offer good guidance, as they do not explicitly require a specific intent or purpose when discerning market manipulation violations involving electronic methods, such as algorithmic and high-frequency trading strategies.

From a comparative perspective, the Korean regime for market manipulation has developed through the adoption and application of regulatory instruments from other major jurisdictions, notably the US. And more recently, Korea has embraced a regulatory approach akin to that of the European Union, exemplified by the EU MAR, which stresses the role of administrative sanctions (in particular, civil monetary penalties). The policy move is largely driven by concerns about effective law enforcement, which predominantly relies on criminal sanctions necessitating rigorous demonstration of the defendant's culpability beyond a reasonable doubt. However, despite such efforts, the evaluation of the Korean market abuse regime indicates that it maintains the *status quo*, steadfastly supporting its existing 'two-tiered hierarchical' system of law enforcement. The principle of 'criminal punishment first' for market abuse offences still firmly holds, potentially undermining efficacy of enforceability as well as predictability of the anti-manipulation regime in Korea. As such, the Korean market manipulation law needs revision, aiming at abolishing the current defective 'dual-track' enforcement system in favour of instituting a more coherent integration regime.

Additionally, in contrast to the US and the EU legislation, the Korean law is silent on high-frequency algorithmic trading regulations. As noted earlier, technology developments of financial markets have dramatically transformed landscapes of securities trading, and the involvement of HFT traders expanded the opportunities for market manipulation. Nevertheless, Korean regulators extensively rely on business regulations set forth by a self-regulatory organisation (KRX) for oversight of activities related to AT and HFT, without a statute specifically directed at market manipulation thereof. Given the limited utility of internal rules of an exchange, market authorities should possess the capability to directly impose regulatory obligations and suitable sanctions on covered persons. As a matter of course, revisions to the Capital Markets Act are required to this end.

Bibliography

Allen, Franklin and Douglas Gale, 'Stock-Price Manipulation' (1992) 5(3) Rev Financ Stud 503.

Avgouleas, Emilios E., 'The Mechanics of Market Manipulation' in *The Mechanics and Regulation of Market Abuse: A Legal and Economic Analysis* (Oxford, 2005; online edn, Oxford Academic, 2010).

Bagot, Sébastien, 'A new European Framework: MAR and CSMAD' (9 November 2016) https://ec.europa.eu/assets/agri/market-sectors/cereals/commodity-expert-group/2016-11-09/dgfisma-bagot-overview-new-eu-legal-framework.pdf.

Balp, Gaia and Giovanni Strampelli, 'Preserving Capital Markets Efficiency in the High-Frequency Trading Era' (2018) 2018(2) U Ill J L Tech & Pol'y 349.

Bell, Holly A and Harrison Searles, 'An Analysis of Global HFT Regulation – Motivations, Market Failures, and Alternative Outcomes' (1 April 2014) *Mercatus Center Working Paper* No 14-11 http://dx.doi.org/10.2139/ssrn.2689321.

Bergþórsson, Andri Fannar, *What is Market Manipulation? An Analysis of the Concept in a European and Nordic Context* in Brill Research Perspectives in International Banking and Securities Law (Brill 2018).

Binder, Eckhard, 'Review of the Benchmark Regulation: to address the phasing-out of the London Interbank Offered Rate (LIBOR) index' *European Parliamentary Research Service Briefing* (October 2020) https://www.europarl.europa.eu/RegData/etudes/BRIE/2020/654187/EPRS_BRI(2020)654187_EN.pdf.

Bridegan, Tyler and Dina Moussa, '*U.S.* v. *Sarao*: The Flash Crash and A New Effort to Prosecute Market Manipulation and Deceptive Trading Practices' (2017) 1(2) Geo L Tech Rev 396.

Busch, Danny, 'MiFID II: regulating high frequency trading, other forms of algorithmic trading and direct electronic market access' (2016) 10(2) Law Financ Mark Rev 72.

Clifford, Anita, 'Double Jeopardy and Concurrent Proceedings for Financial Wrongdoing' *Lexology Article* (11 September 2017) https://www.lexology.com/library/detail.aspx?g=3d69e4fe-c92c-4fb1-88b6-1ea4057a6405.

Coffee Jr, John C, 'Paradigms Lost: The Blurring of the Criminal and Civil Law Models – And What Can Be Done About It' (1992) 101(8) Yale L J 1875.

Commodity Futures Trading Commission (CFTC), Remarks of Commissioner Bart Chilton to Metals Market Investors, Washington, D.C. (23 March 2010) https://www.cftc.gov/PressRoom/SpeechesTestimony/opachilton-30.

Commodity Futures Trading Commission (CFTC), 'Fact Sheet: Anti-Manipulation and Anti-Fraud Final Rules' (14 July 2011) https://www.cftc.gov/sites/default/files/idc/groups/public/@newsroom/documents/file/amaf_factsheet_final.pdf.

Commodity Futures Trading Commission (CFTC), 'Fact Sheet: Interpretive Guidance and Policy Statement on Disruptive practices' (28 May 2013) https://www.cftc.gov/sites/default/files/idc/groups/public/@newsroom/documents/file/dtp_factsheet.pdf.

Commodity Futures Trading Commission (CFTC), 'A Proposed Rule: Concept Release on Risk Controls and System Safeguards for Automated Trading Environments' 78 Fed Reg 56542 (12 September 2013).

Cosme Jr., Orlando, 'Regulating High-Frequency Trading: The Case for Individual Criminal Liability' (2019) 109(2) J Crim. L & Criminology 365.

DeFranco, Thomas P. and others, 'SEC v. Jarkesy: Supreme Court Delivers Significant Blow to SEC Intra-Agency Enforcement' *Insights* (8 July 2024) https://www.dwt.com/blogs/financial-services-law-advisor/2024/07/takeaways-from-scotus-ruling-in-sec-v-jarkesy.

European Central Bank (ECB), 'Algorithmic trading: trends and existing regulation' *Newsletter articles* (13 February 2019) https://www.bankingsupervision.europa.eu/press/publications/newsletter/2019/html/ssm.nl190213_5.en.html.

European Securities and Markets Authority (ESMA), Report on Suspicious Transaction and Order Reports (STORS) (17 July 2023) https://www.esma.europa.eu/press-news/esma-news/esma-publishes-report-suspicious-transactions-and-order-reports.

Financial Industry Regulatory Authority (FINRA), '2022 Report on FINRA's Examination and Risk Monitoring Program' (9 February 2022) https://www.finra.org/rules-guidance/guidance/reports/2022-finras-examination-and-risk-monitoring-program/market-access-rule.

Financial Services Commission (FSC), Press Release: the Cabinet passed a partial amendment of the Financial Investment Services and Capital Markets Act to prohibit market disturbances (23 December 2014).

Financial Services Commission (FSC), Press Release: Implementation of the Comprehensive Measures to Eradicate Illegal Activities for the Sound Development of the Securities Market (19 October 2020).

Financial Services Commission (FSC), Press Release: Measures to Strengthen Capacity to Respond to Unfair Trade Practices in Capital Markets (28 September 2022).

Financial Services Commission (FSC), Press Release: SFC Imposes Penalty Surcharge on Overseas-based Financial Investment Entity for Market Disturbance (26 January 2023).

Fischel, Daniel R. and David J. Ross, 'Should the Law Prohibit Manipulation in Financial Markets?' (1991) 105(2) Harv L Rev 503.

Fox, Merritt B., Lawrence R. Glosten and Gabriel V. Rauterberg, 'The New Stock Market: Sense and Nonsense' (2015) 65(2) Duke L J 191.

Fox, Merritt. B., Lawrence R. Glosten and Gabriel V. Rauterberg, 'Stock Market Manipulation and Its Regulation' (2018) 35(1) Yale J Reg 67.

HM Treasury, Policy statement – Building a smarter financial services framework for the UK (December 2022) https://assets.publishing.service.gov.uk/media/6391d6128fa8f53bac58e476/Building_a_smarter_financial_services_framework_for_the_UK_.pdf.

Im Chool Park, 'A Study on Unfair Transactions under Article 178 of the Financial Investment Services and Capital Markets Act' (2013) 14(2) Korean J Secur Law 353.

International Organisation of Securities Commissions (IOSCO), Investigating and Prosecuting Market Manipulation, Report of the Technical Committee of the IOSCO (May 2000) https://www.iosco.org/library/pubdocs/pdf/IOSCOPD103.pdf.

International Organisation of Securities Commissions (IOSCO), Addendum to IOSCO Report on Investigating and Prosecuting Market Manipulation (April 2013) https://www.iosco.org/library/pubdocs/pdf/IOSCOPD411.pdf.

Kahan, Marcel, 'Securities Law and the Social Costs of Inaccurate Stock Prices' (1992) 41(5) Duke L J 977.

Kang, Min-woo, 'Enforcing the market abuse regime in Korea: recent developments and challenges ahead' (2021) 16(4) Cap Mark Law J 528.

Kang, Min-woo, 'Theories of Causal Nexus in Rule 10b-5 Claims: A Critical Reassessment' (2022) 2(1) L Bus 5.

Korsmo, Charles R, 'High-frequency Trading: A Regulatory Strategy' (2014) 48(2) U Rich L Rev, 523.

Korea Exchange (KRX), Press Release: Notice of Revision of Securities and Derivatives Market Business Regulations to Manage High-Speed Algorithmic Traders (25 October 2022).

Kyle, Albert S. and S. Viswanathan, 'How to Define Illegal Price Manipulation' (2008) 98(2) Am Econ Rev 274.

Ledgerwood, Shaun D., and Paul R. Carpenter, 'A Framework for the Analysis of Market Manipulation' (2012) 8(1) Rev L & Econ 253.

Lee, Jihoon, 'S. Korea fines Citadel Securities for stock algorithm trading breaches' *Reuters* (27 January 2023) https://www.reuters.com/business/finance/skorea-fines-citadel-securities-stock-algorithm-trading-breaches-2023-01-27/.

Lee, Jung Soo, 'A Research on a Stock Manipulation through Actual Trading: Interpretational Approach and Complementary Measures to the Act' (2020) 33(1) Commer Case Law 167.

Lee, Jung Soo, 'A Research on the Direction of Legislative Improvement for the Market Abuse Rule' (2023) 24(1) Korean J Secur Law 93.

Lerch, Marus, 'Algorithmic Trading and High-Frequency Trading' in Rüdiger Veil (ed), European Capital Markets Law (3rd edn, Hart 2022).

Lin, Tom C., 'New Market Manipulation' (2017) 66(6) Emory L J 1253.

Mackintosh, Phil, 'All about LULDS' *NASDAQ News & Insights* (10 February 2022) https://www.nasdaq.com/articles/all-about-lulds.

Mann, Ronald, 'Justices limit major SEC tool to penalise fraud' SCOTUSblog – *Opinion Analysis* (28 June 2024) https://www.scotusblog.com/case-files/cases/securities-and-exchange-commission-v-jarkesy/.

Markham, Jerry W., *Law Enforcement and the History of Financial Market Manipulation* (Routledge 2015).

Moore, James W.M. and Frank M. Wiseman, 'Market Manipulation and the Exchange Act' (1934) 2(1) U Chi L Rev 46.

Morelli, Michael, 'Implementing High Frequency Trading Regulation: A Critical Analysis of Current Reforms' (2017) 6(2) Mich Bus & Entrepreneurial L Rev 201.

Multer, Maxwell K., 'Open-Market Manipulation Under SEC Rule 10b-5 and its Analogues: Inappropriate Distinctions, Judicial Disagreement and Case Study: FERC's Anti-Manipulation Rule', (2011) 39(2) SEC REG L J 97.

Perrone, Andrea, 'EU Market Abuse Regulation: The Puzzle of Enforcement' (2020) 21(2) Eur Bus Organ L Rev 379.

Political Affairs Committee, *A Draft on Partially Amended Financial Investment Services and Capital Markets Act* (Bill No 2122985, June 2023).

Political Affairs Committee, *Review Report on Partially Amended Financial Investment Services and Capital Markets Act* (Bill No 2103921, June 2023).

Press Release: Federal Regulators Finalise Tough New Market Manipulation Rule Required by Cantwell (7 July 2011) https://www.cantwell.senate.gov/news/press-releases/federal-regulators-finalize-tough-new-market-manipulation-rule-required-by-cantwell.

Poser, Norman S., 'Stock Market Manipulation and Corporate Control Transactions' (1986) 40(3) U Miami L Rev 671.

Putniņš, Tālis J., 'Market Manipulation: A Survey' (2012) 26(5) Journal of Economic Surveys 952.

Ravelli, Rahman, 'A Primer on Market Manipulation Regulations in the US and UK' (January 2021) https://www.rahmanravelli.co.uk/assets/Resource-Guides/Market-Manipulation/92edfae54c/Market-Manipulation-Master-Guide-29-Jan-2021.pdf.

Robson, Niel, 'The CSMAD: significant imminent changes to EU market abuse and insider dealing rules' *Financier Worldwide Expert Briefing* (May 2015) https://www.financierworldwide.com/the-csmad-significant-imminent-changes-to-eu-market-abuse-and-insider-dealing-rules.

Sagayam, Selina, 'New European Market Abuse Regime – What Do Non-EU Incorporated Issuers Need to Know?' *GIBSON DUNN Client Alert* (22 June 2016) https://www.gibsondunn.com/new-european-market-abuse-regime-what-do-non-eu-incorporated-issuers-need-to-know/.

Securities and Exchange Commission (SEC), 'Concept Rule: Short Sales' Release Number 34–42037; File Number S7-24-99 (28 October 1999).

Securities and Exchange Commission (SEC), 'Final Rule: Risk Management Controls for Brokers or Dealers with Market Access' Release No. 34-63241; File No. S7-03-10 (3 November 2010) https://www.sec.gov/files/rules/final/2010/34-63241.pdf.

Securities and Exchange Commission (SEC), Press Release: SEC Approves New Rules Prohibiting Market Maker Stub Quotes (8 November 2010) https://www.sec.gov/news/press/2010/2010-216.htm.

Securities and Exchange Commission (SEC), 'Updated Investor Alert: Social Media and Investing – Stock Rumours' *Investor Alerts and Bulletins* (5 November 2015) https://www.sec.gov/oiea/investor-alerts-bulletins/ia-rumors.

Spicer, Jonathan, 'FACTBOX: After the flash crash, changes to U.S. markets' *Reuters* (18 February 2011) https://www.reuters.com/article/financial-regulation-flashcrash-idUSN1827676320110218.

Thel, Steve, 'The Original Conception of Section 10(b) of the Securities Exchange Act' (1990) 42(2) Stan L Rev 385.

Tountopoulos, Vassilios D., 'Market Abuse and Private Enforcement' (2014) 11(3) Eur Co Financial Law Rev 297.

Veil, Rüdiger, 'Market Manipulation' in Rüdiger Veil (ed), *European Capital Markets Law* (3rd edn, Hart 2022).

Woodward, Megan, 'The Need for Speed: Regulatory Approaches to High Frequency Trading in the United States and the European Union' (2021) 50 Vanderbilt Law Rev 1359.

Yang, GiJin, 'Limitations and Improvement Plans of Regulation of Market Manipulative Behaviours using High Frequency Algorithm under the Current Korean Law' (2023) 13(2) J Fin Consum 107.

Zahabi, Erza and others, 'Beginning of the End of EU Law in the UK?' *Akin Insights: Alerts* (13 July 2023) https://www.akingump.com/a/web/n7bAeiFLoMkGKhT77MSi3w/7Z7Dez/beginning-of-the-end-of-eu-law-in-the-uk-v4.pdf.

www.ingramcontent.com/pod-product-compliance
Lightning Source LLC
Chambersburg PA
CBHW031333230926
51848CB00001B/220